I HOPE

RAISA
GORBACHEV

I HOPE

Translated by David Floyd

HarperCollins*Publishers*

FIRST EDITION

Library of Congress Cataloging-in-Publication Data

Gorbacheva, Raisa Maksimovna.
    I hope : reminiscences and reflections / Raisa Gorbachev : translated
by David Floyd.
      p. cm.
    ISBN 0-06-016852-8
    1. Gorbacheva, Raisa Maksimovna. 2. Heads of state—Soviet Union—Wives—
Autobiography. 3. Soviet Union— Politics and government—1985- . I. Priakhin,
G. V. (Georgii V.) II. Title.
DK290.3.G675A3 1991
947.085'4'092—dc20
[B]   91-57919

---

91 92 93 94 95 HC 10 9 8 7 6 5 4 3 2 1

Raisa Gorbachev
tells of herself, of her past and her present
in conversation
with writer Georgi Pryakhin

Contents

TRANSLATOR'S NOTE   ix

TO THE FOREIGN READER   xi

1   Invitation to an Interview   1

2   We Were All Children Once   11

3   University Years   41

4   The Test of Real Life   75

5   Things I Take to Heart   129

6   My Hopes   196

Translator's Note

For the sake of clarity the words spoken by the Interviewer, Georgi Pryakhin, are printed in italics throughout.

To the Foreign Reader

I have explained in the first chapter of my book, entitled 'Invitation to an Interview', the motives that prompted me to take up my pen and write this book. I can add to what I have already said only this: for the last few years I have resolutely rejected all the offers I have had to write a book or to give interviews about myself and my family. But now that I have decided to do so my decision is just as firm. This probably happens with many people, and so it has happened with me.

My book *I Hope* had a short gestation – just four months. It is not a book of memoirs or an autobiography with its scrupulous attention to chronology and detail. Still less is it a systematic exposition of my views and beliefs, although they are present in the book. It is a book of straight speaking, probably at times inconsistent, emotional and patchy. It is a story about myself in the past and in the present, about events and impressions gained on the spot. It is a spontaneous and particularly personal response to what is happening around me and to the dramatic conflicts, shocks and, nevertheless, accomplishments that now distinguish public life in my country.

For me this book provides an opportunity to express myself, to explain certain things and to put to rest certain misunderstandings. It also enables me to share my problems, my anxieties and my hopes. If that finds a response in your hearts I will be happy.

As for the form the book takes, it seemed to me that, bearing in mind all the circumstances I have mentioned, the most natural form would be a live conversation.

RAISA GORBACHEV
June 1991

CHAPTER ONE

Invitation to an Interview

I might very well have got to know back in 1964 the wife of the man who was to become the first Soviet President. She was then living near me — a couple of hundred kilometres from the small town where, left at an early age without parents, I was brought up, first in a children's home and later in a school for working-class boys where every other classmate was nearly twice my age and weight. It was there that I began my career as a reporter. At times the future 'first lady' would come a lot closer to our town as she made her way through the daunting sea of mud that the country roads turned into in the autumn. She was then probing into the depths of village life, pursuing her sociological surveys.

Like a good agronomist, a real village sociologist has chosen a foot-slogging career. I have before me at the moment a booklet made of poor-quality faded paper published in 1967, on which is written: 'R. M. Gorbachev. Summary of thesis submitted in support of an application for the degree of doctor of philosophy'. It is entitled The Development of New Features in the Life of the Peasantry in Collective Farms.

This frail researcher would make her way round the villages in her rubber boots — try to lift your boot out of the mud and your foot in its thick woollen sock comes out of the boot — because at that time there was no other way of getting round the villages as they were then. She would drink tea with the old women and war widows. A truly foot-slogging profession, that of a village sociologist! But she was hardly likely to have used the unfamiliar term 'sociologist' to introduce herself in those days. She probably used other words, more intelligible to the country folk.

It was, however, many years later and a long way from those places that we got to know each other. It was in Moscow that it happened.

And now a few days ago I received an unexpected invitation to act as a sort of interviewer for a book largely of a biographical nature. Today I was invited to the President's suburban residence. It turned out not to be a long journey . . .

Once through the gate the car swept round the driveway, skirting a wood, probably planted many years ago, a 'bright' plantation of trees, as we Russians say. The thick tops of the spruce and firs and the branches of the limes made patterns against the darkening sky, and the older, rugged limes were sunk deep in the undisturbed snow. Beyond the trees I caught sight of a compact yellow two-storey building that reminded me of a country house of the end of the last century. The Volga braked to a halt and I stepped out and saw Raisa Maksimovna Gorbachev standing in the wide double glass doors.

She was wearing a patterned sweater, probably knitted at home. I had already seen her once in that sweater — at the central republican children's hospital which she supported and which she had visited some days previously quite informally and had spent more than three hours there. I'd not seen her wearing trousers. The sweater, the trousers and the slippers with cloth tops suited the lady of the house. 'Hello,' she said, stretching out her hand from the threshold.

Her look was attentive and welcoming.

There was nothing very striking about the hall: indeed it was rather too functional. To the left, inside the house, was a cloak-room. My overcoat looked rather lonely there. Below the hooks were some house-shoes. All the same, I didn't change my shoes. We went up to the first floor by steep, spotlessly clean stairs. There were some framed pictures hanging on the wall. My hostess pointed to one of them:

How do you like this owl? People send me as mementoes whatever they can, whatever they can do, especially children. So they sent me the owl. I asked for it to be hung here. I believe the owl is the symbol of tranquillity and wisdom. Isn't that so?

I was not sure about wisdom, but the owl on the wall was good-natured and anything but grey. It was immediately apparent that the little person who drew it made use of every single colour that came to hand.

We went into the library and then into the President's study, which turned out to be much smaller than might have been expected. It was an ordinary room but beautifully panelled in wood. Two things struck me immediately as I crossed the threshold — the bright red, oddly shaped telephone beneath a transparent cover, and an enlarged photograph in a frame standing in a gap between the bookshelves. As for the telephone, I immediately realized, of course, the sort of telephone it was, to judge by its striking colour. As for the large framed portrait, I could not immediately place it.

The President resembles his mother far more than he does his father — that is what I realized a moment later.

The enlarged photograph was of a man with a contented smile, as if after long and hard labours, and a thinning tuft of hair. His tunic, open at the neck, was quite worn out — that was clear even in a black-and-white photo. Rows of medals hung on his broad chest. The soldier in the photo had seen life, as they say. He was obviously well over twenty. He was one of the workhorses who had borne the brunt of the war and after. The photo looked as if it had been taken just after the end of the war.

The bright red telephone and the enlarged photograph are facing one another. When the President is sitting in his chair at his desk he probably exchanges glances with his father, now sadly dead.

Books in glass-fronted cases covered the walls from top to bottom in the library and the study. I made an effort to remember the titles — perhaps I would have to write about them some day. There were beautiful volumes on Russian history — Solovyev, Karamzin, Klyuchevsky . . . Through one of the doors I noticed a strip of paper stuck to a shelf with writing on it: 'Friends — please arrange these alphabetically . . .' My hostess said with a smile:

'In this room I am secretary and librarian and filing clerk all in one. I try to bring some order into things.'

I can't be quite sure, but I was possibly the first member of the Soviet Union of Writers to examine the President's library. In a corner on a shelf behind a pile of books I noticed a postcard in colour with an inscription in French.

Nikolai Benois. A memento.

The preliminary, improvised excursion was over. If I try hard I can name only two things that might be called luxuries: the desk in the library with its top made of Karelian birch — very impressive and official-looking — and the cleanliness. It was that zealous, living, almost sweet-smelling cleanliness that hovered in the air and seemed vaguely to recall the cleanliness of the village houses in Southern Russia, a resemblance probably evoked also by the photo of the soldier, badly wounded but still returned from the war — it is a rare home in Russia that does not have such a picture. The windows had beautifully hung net curtains. My hostess drew the curtain back for me to look. A little distance from the window, half hidden in the twilight, the trees could be seen in silhouette. The garden?

The garden . . . the 10th of March, 1985. The day Konstantin Ustinovich Chernenko died. At 10 o'clock in the evening there was a specially summoned meeting of the Politburo. Mikhail Sergeyevich returned home very late — we were then living in the country house near Moscow. We went out into the garden. There was something oppressive in the late-night air, still untouched by the spring. Three deaths in three years. The death of three General Secretaries, the country's top leaders, one after the other. Mikhail Sergeyevich was very tired. At first he remained silent. Then he said: 'Tomorrow there will be a full meeting of the Central Committee. The question may arise of my taking over the leadership of the party.' This was completely unexpected news for me. It was to some degree a shock. More than that. I realized that it was also a surprise for my husband. And we had never previously discussed this subject together.

We strolled around the garden where the snow was still lying. My husband again remained silent. Then he appeared quietly to be thinking aloud. 'I worked so many years in Stavropol. This is my seventh year in Moscow. But it is impossible to achieve anything substantial, anything on a large scale, the things the country is waiting for. It's like coming up against a wall. Yet life demands it and has done for a long time. No!' I heard him say. 'We just can't go on like this.'

That was the first time I heard those words.

We had been sitting for a long time at a small polished table. The tape recorder was switched on. I had my pen and notebook in my hands. I could see that my interlocutor had undoubtedly been preparing for today's meeting. But those preparations had nothing elaborate about them. She did not have even a notebook, only odd pieces of paper. They were pages pulled out of a notebook and from an ordinary school exercise book, folded in half or quarters with sometimes a complete page of white writing paper mixed up in a bundle. She would take out the next piece of paper which might have just one sentence written on it, glance at it for a moment, as people glance thoughtfully at a playing-card, read out the words when she had decyphered them, and, putting her notes aside, develop the thought she had written down. There was nothing zealously methodical about her summary notes or about her reminiscences themselves. It was done and recorded in a hurry. I imagine it works like this: something comes to mind in the course of the day's activities, some thought she has been groping for suddenly comes to the surface, and she quickly makes a note of it on the first thing that comes to hand. If it is true that the style makes the man, then in this case the pieces of paper reflect the style, not just of a way of thinking but of a life far from being without cares.

So that was the first time I heard those words. Today they are repeated by millions of people and whole legends have grown up around them. I suppose one can say that that night marked the beginning of a new phase that brought radical changes into the life of our country and my life too.

The *perestroika* years . . . What have they given us? A great deal. The democratization of every aspect of our life. The advent of new thinking in international affairs. As I have accompanied the President on trips in this country and abroad the most important thing I have detected in the sea of human emotions and good wishes is the newly born faith in the possibility of living without war.

The *perestroika* years have given us much. And at the same time very little. It is hard for our country now, very hard. There are problems that have been building up for decades and maybe for centuries. The difficulty of finding new ways. The shortage of consumer goods. And again, something very important: In the words of Dostoevsky, in a time of troubles and change you always get all sorts of 'dirt' everywhere. Unfortunately our *perestroika* has not been able to avoid that dangerous, destructive and corrosive 'dirt'. How could it be otherwise? On the whole, it is a time of hopes and alarms, of achievements and failures. A time for thoughts and doubts.

It is difficult to talk about oneself. It is always difficult, I suppose, for everyone. But today it seems particularly difficult for me to do so.

The telephone rang. I guessed it was not the red one. That probably had a different tone. And in any case it couldn't ring in the absence of the man in whose study it stood. Its tone certainly followed him around, on his heels wherever he happened to be – in his study, in his car or at some political meeting.

How are you feeling, Mikhail Sergeyevich? Tired?

I did not hear the reply, if only because I rose and went quietly from the study to the library.

It is difficult to talk about oneself. I have already had repeated proposals from various newspapers and magazines to give them an interview. And from publishers, including American ones, requests to produce a book about myself. I have not done so. And, to tell you the truth, I never thought of doing it. I neither did it nor thought of doing it. For various reasons, primarily subjective ones. It always seemed to me to be quite unnecessary. I say this quite sincerely. Why should I talk about myself? Just about me? I am not a film star or a writer or an artist or a musician or a fashion designer. And I am not a politician. I am not a statesman who has to take major decisions and be responsible for people's fate. I am the wife of the head of the Soviet state, supporting my husband as far as I can and helping him as I have always done ever since our young days when we linked our lives together. In our family we have always had, and still have, this understanding: the problem of each member of the family is everybody's problem.

In 1985, because of Mikhail Sergeyevich's journeys and the visits paid to us by the heads of other states, a problem arose. It is the tradition in other countries for the wives of leaders to take part in various public and formal occasions. This was not the practice of our predecessors. What were we to do? Mikhail Sergeyevich said: 'Let everything happen naturally.' So, quite naturally, we began to adopt the practice, accepted throughout the rest of the world: the wife of the leader of the state began to appear in public. It is just another sign of the 'liberalization' introduced by *perestroika*, though it was far from being the most important.

The way I behave now and the way my husband and I behave today is the natural continuation of the relationship between us, our careers and our lives. We have certainly not thought up anything 'special' because of our new duties. So, I ask myself again, is there any need to write about me, or for me to talk about myself? After all, what is most important is the cause for which Mikhail Sergeyevich, his colleagues and supporters are working: that – his cause – is what essentially determines my manner of life today.

And again, it was not the practice in our country for the wives of top leaders to give interviews or write books, especially about themselves. This may appear to a Western reader to be a prejudiced view. But prejudices can also be traditions, and it presumably behoves the wife of the President to observe the traditions to an even greater extent than the President himself, especially in such matters.

Nevertheless I am in this case breaking the sort of 'vow of silence' that I have kept since 1985. I have been brought to this by the logic of life and pushed into it by the meetings and contacts I have had with people, and by the lively and quite genuine, and I would say grateful, interest in our affairs today which are being followed so keenly throughout the world. And finally the problem of 'Soviet Woman and perestroika' and the questions put to me, including those in so many letters. Among the innumerable meetings that led me gradually to think about producing a book were those that took place in America. First in 1987 and then in the summer of 1990 when I made a trip with Mrs Barbara Bush to visit a women's college where the girls showered me with questions. That finally changed my mind.

Moreover it was in those years, around the world and in our own country, that quite a lot of material, articles and even books about me appeared in which goodwill was by no means always accompanied by knowledge of the facts, and on occasion accuracy was totally absent, and invention, myths and even slander became the 'basis' of what was written. Certain authors will forgive me for saying this, but if it had not been for my name appearing in the text I would never have believed that they were writing about me.

It was then that I decided that I would tell my story, about my understanding of life, about what I have lived through, about what was close and dear to me. To speak to those who are willing to listen. To recount and to talk. I have invited you, Georgi Vladimirovich, to be my interviewer.

She put the piece of paper aside. There was a pause.

'Perhaps we should explain why the choice fell on me?' I asked, although I did not know what the reason was — which is why I asked.

Well, for one reason, because I know you. Because you were born in Stavropol, where Mikhail Sergeyevich was also born. And, finally, because you have four daughters in your family. Therefore you are a humane and good person. Is that enough?'

'Plenty, in my view.'

No. The most important thing is that all your children are living with you. That tells me a great deal.

'Thank you,' I said, although I admit it was the first time I had been praised for that. Truth to tell, the family often criticizes me for not improving our lot — seven people in a single flat makes life difficult. A pity they don't hear.

My notebook is full. The tape recorder has been switched off. Tea has been drunk. Outside, beyond the net curtains at the window there is complete darkness. We put everything back in its place in the President's study — the table and the two chairs. The cut-glass vase is moved from the President's desk to a low side-table. In parting I glance round the room once more. Next to the photograph of his father is a slightly smaller one of his wife, taken early in their marriage. It is the face of a young girl with a very concentrated, highly attentive expression, looking straight ahead but still seeming to be turned in upon herself.

That was the year I finished university. Do you know what struck me recently? I am wearing a grey jacket and a dark red blouse. Can you believe it? Yet they still talk of a lack of constancy in women's character.

Grey is one of her favourite colours. The same grey colour that the author Ivan Bunin defined in his elegant way as being not grey at all but 'pearly'. Pearly-grey.

But the photograph is a black-and-white one! That means she could remember both the jacket and the blouse. It was what she wore as a student after the war, and like the rest of us she had no difficulty in recalling it.

We went down by the same wooden staircase. In the very functional hallway I notice something I had for some reason not noticed before. It was a little decorated doll's house with a toboggan next to it. It was a very touching reminder of the New Year seen in very official premises.

That is a completely private house in a state residence. It belongs to the grandchildren. I'm afraid they are both down with colds at the moment.

I left in the same car by the same entrance. The soldier standing beneath the light at the gate saluted as I departed. He was the only soldier I saw at the residence. In fact, I saw only three people altogether: the man on the gate, my hostess and a charming woman who served the tea and whom the President's wife with Russian simplicity and friendliness addressed as 'Shura'.

On the way back into Moscow we did not meet a car returning with the President. It was eight o'clock — too early for him to be coming home.

CHAPTER TWO

We Were All Children Once

Raisa Maksimovna, I have already guessed that you like Antoine de Saint-Exupéry and I have heard you quote more than once passages from Le Petit Prince. *I will begin our conversation today with a well-known quotation from Exupéry: 'We were all children once . . .'*

Yes, I love him and the little fellow he created who performed such great and good deeds. Childhood is a world of fantasy and dreams. A time for thousands of questions. And the first attempts to find answers to them. Every one of us had a childhood. And then, when we were children, it seemed as though there could be no other childhood. That is how it remains dear to us.

We went to school, then to pioneer groups and then to young Communist meetings. We were proud of our country's achievements – Magnitka, Dneproges, Komsomolsk on the Amur, the voyage of the *Chelyuskin*, Valeri Chkalov, Valentina Grizodubova. We admired the heroism of Alexander Matrosov, Zoya Kosmodemyanskaya, the Young Guards. We read every book that came to hand. We dreamt about long journeys, faraway countries and cities. My dream was to be the captain of an ocean-going ship . . . We dreamt of finding treasure. We were always seeking for treasure!

Today my young ones dream mostly about meeting creatures from other planets.

No, we never lost hope and went on stubbornly looking for treasure. Then, of course, we played war games. I know all children play at war in one way or another. But for the children of my generation playing at war had very painful associations – often it was too close to reality. Of course, we played at schools and with our dolls, but what stays in my mind is playing at war. Each of us, of course, wanted to be a partisan, Chapayev or Anka, and, if they weren't given any other 'positive' role, even the little boys were willing to be Anka, the girl from the film *Chapayev*. No one wanted to be a White, or a German or a Fascist. It didn't occur to us that those same Whites, for example, were also our fellow countrymen.

Yes, as I look back now over the years and reflect on my childhood and my generation, and as I study, for example, the photographs I was looking through before you arrived, the most important thing I recall is war. It followed us everywhere. War in Spain. Detachments of volunteers. The Finnish war. The clash with Japanese troops in Khalkin-Gol. And within the country too? The 1930s and the 'enemies of the people'. I remember how, in the first and second grades at school the pictures of Yegorov, Blyukher, Tukhachevsky* were blotted out in our text-books. I feel sad, bitter recalling it.

And then, finally, the Patriotic War of '41 to '45. Millions of lives lost, millions of lives ruined. Houses laid waste, families orphaned, towns and villages destroyed, scorched earth . . . Crowds swarming the railway stations. The country was turned into one big railway station. It seemed as though there were only two emotions prevailing – parting and waiting. Faces swollen from hunger. And the feeling of fear – of losing your food ration card or your bread ration. I remember it to this very day. And gleaning the fields for ears of grain and frozen potatoes. That is the way it was. For me and for all my age group.

Then came the joy of victory. That had to be experienced.

* Military leaders executed in the Purge of 1937.

The happiness of welcoming those close and related to you back home and alive. And, altogether, that overwhelming feeling of the joy of being alive, just, you know, being physically alive.

My father was born in 1907 and was a Ukrainian. My mother, born in 1913, is Russian, a native of Siberia.

Georgi Vladimirovich, we agreed that there would be no precise or strict logical order in my observations, didn't we? I would rather describe them as a mosaic, spoken on impulse. Things that sprang to mind and fitted in with my current mood. These are not memoirs, isn't that so?

That is exactly what I like about them – that they are not memoirs. And I like the fact that you react emotionally when you recall your childhood and those years and do not simply set them out unemotionally on their shelves.

My father worked throughout his life on the railway system. Whenever I filled in questionnaires I always wrote: father a railway employee. Non-Party. Oh yes, non-Party. Faith in the Party came to my father along with Mikhail Sergeyevich, my husband. Despite the difference in their ages, my husband became for him a symbol of what a Communist should be. My father arrived in Siberia in the spring of 1929. He was born in Chernigov but came to Siberia in 1929.

Where exactly did he move to?

He came to work on building the railway. The first railway my father built was the one from Rubtsovsk to Ridder in the Altai. His parents – his father Andrei Filippovich and his mother Maria Maksimovna – abandoned their land in the village and went to live in the town, Chernigov. They left the land because they couldn't feed themselves from it. My father went with his comrades in search of work to the West Siberian region, as it was then called. It is now the Altai region. He found work building the railway, which was actually to run through the village where my mother was born – Veseloyarsk. Oh yes, there is such a village – I just received a letter with New Year greetings from there.

Mikhail Sergeyevich said of me in the course of an interview that I was born in Siberia, in the Altai region, in Rubtsovsk. So the people there began to take an interest in me and my mother. I am touched by that well-meaning interest. And so it was in Veseloyarsk that my parents linked their lives. My father carried on building the railway and met his wife in the process.

Veseloyarsk is a nice name. There aren't so many such names in our country. For some reason we don't like to draw attention to what is best in the character of our towns and villages – is it part of our national character? Sometimes when you are travelling you read the names of the places and can be really put off by them – Gryaznukha, say, or Cherny Yar . . . But here we have Veseloyarsk.*

Gogol also pointed that out.

I was the first child in the family. I was christened in accordance with the Orthodox tradition. Not in church, of course – what sort of church could there be then in 1932 at the very height of the struggle against the Church – but in a priest's home. True, my name was not taken out of the Church calendar. As you know, the tradition was for the priest to propose a name that he found in the calendar. But it was my parents who chose my name. My father chose it. It is well known how many beautiful national Slav and Russian names we have. But at that time new names were being invented. New names for new times. Among people of my age lots were called Oktyabrina referring to the October Revolution and Vladilena referring to Vladimir Lenin. And new names were appearing among the better-educated – Nelly, Jeanne or

* In Russian *gryaznukha* means the dirty place, *cherny yar* means the black hole, and *veseloyarsk* means the happy town.

Alla. But my father named me Raisa – Rayechka. He explained to me later that for him it meant 'rai' – 'paradise'. The apple in the Garden of Eden.

It is also used very widely in my part of the country. But I have never heard such an explanation for it. Your father has a good imagination!

Don't forget that I was the first child. My father was very fond of all his children but nevertheless he was particularly attached to me throughout his life. To his first child. And he was very proud of me. In the last months of his life, when he lay in hospital here in Moscow he told me that for some reason he kept thinking of his mother and of me as a little girl. 'I always knew, always felt that you were the one who would save my life,' he told me in hospital. Unfortunately we did not succeed in saving him for long. He had a complicated operation. In 1986 he died.

To recall myself sitting at his bedside in the hospital and to hear him saying what were in fact his parting words to me evokes too many personal emotions. Perhaps there's no need to talk about it? I would rather not.

Her voice is quiet. Quiet and at the same time distinct. It is easy to imagine her addressing an audience. I know there was a time in Stavropol when students, including some of my friends, were eager to attend her lectures. They are keen to listen to lecturers like her because they are also pleasant to look at, being more or less the same age as the students themselves. But she now uses a different voice from the one that can be heard from time to time on the television. It is the voice of a daughter whose audience is composed essentially of one person – herself.

My mother's parents [*she continues, bringing her voice under control*] Petr Stepanovich and Anastasia Vasilevna were also of a peasant family. Did they have an easy life? Don't you believe it – as my mother tells me now. Don't you believe that peasants were prosperous in the past. It was hard and hopeless labour. The land, the cattle and little to eat. Your poor grandmother! – my mother Aleksandra Petrovna exclaims every time. It was forced labour and not a normal life that she had. She ploughed, sowed, washed the clothes and fed six children. And throughout her life not a word of complaint.

My mother's sister Vera died when she was sixteen. What of? No one knows for sure. After all, there was no medical attention. The eldest brother Aleksandr died when he was twenty-six. Of what? Again, no one knows.

Lenin gave my parents land – that is what my mother always says. Previously they didn't have their own land. They were told, according to my mother, to take as much as they wanted, as much as they could cultivate. But at the beginning of the 1930s my grandfather's family were treated as 'rich peasants', their land and house were taken from them and they had to make a living by casual work. And later, my mother says, grandfather was accused of Trotskyism. He was arrested and disappeared without trace.

Really! Our unpredictable Russian history hangs as heavy as a soldier's greatcoat, soaked in blood. The person sitting opposite me has had a completely different career, a different age and, finally, different 'origins', as they said in olden days. But her grandfather was also expropriated. My grandfather was expropriated and my father shipped from one part of the country to another. Where else can you come across this sort of thing? But in Russia, however painful it may be, you find it at every step.

Yes, don't be surprised. My mother still has no idea who Trotsky was, and my grandfather certainly didn't know. And to this very day my mother cannot understand what her father was accused of. We all lived through this common tragedy. That is why today I am so frightened by the appeals you hear on every side to 'seek out the guilty ones'. It would only lead to another round of bloodshed.

My grandmother died of grief and hunger as the wife of an 'enemy of the people'. And the four children she left behind were left to the mercy of fate.

My grandfather Petr Stepanovich made sure that his sons had a good education. The eldest, Aleksandr, who died at the age of twenty-six, was trained as an economist. The youngest, Ivan, also had an education. But, in the Russian tradition, no special attention was given to the education of the daughters. In peasant homes the women were practically all illiterate. From the age of eight my mother did the ploughing and spinning. It was only after she was married that she attended courses in reading and writing. She helped her younger sister to be trained as a pharmacist. My mother is a person equipped with natural and very sharp intellectual qualities. All her life she regarded the lack of an education as her tragedy. So she saw it as her main purpose in life to provide her own children with a proper upbringing. And she did in fact give all her children a good education.

My mother did not go out to work: she remained a house-wife. The never-ending moves the family had to make in the wake of my father the railwayman, the trouble that this caused, the various flats we found to live in — goodness knows how many such 'nests' we occupied, and huts and wooden-frame houses . . . Although we did have one beautiful large wooden house in the Urals. Our family was given it in the war years, by what good luck I no longer remember. And for some time we had an 'apartment' in the buildings of a former monastery. So can you imagine what our life was like? That was the war. And even after the war our family lived as before, like birds of passage. It was only after forty years of work that my father and mother were provided with a permanent place to live, and even then with great difficulty.

My mother remained a housewife also because by the time she was twenty-five she already had three children. But I can't remember a time, from childhood to the present day, when my mother was not busy at something or other, when she would sit and rest for a while. Throughout her life, her whole life, she was always sewing, mending, darning, knitting, cooking, embroidering or cleaning. She mended everything herself, kept everything tidy, worked in the garden and, when it was possible, kept a cow or a goat so that the children could have milk. And she is still the same today, despite her years.

In character my mother is strict and demanding. I remember the scene when we accompanied my father off to the front. The overcrowded railway station – I really do recall from childhood so clearly and so sharply the railway stations with that unrepeatable sad atmosphere – women, children and tears. Many women even fainted. And I remember my mother, frozen in her grief. Her words were: 'Who's going to support us? We must hold out.'

We saw our father off to the front, but he didn't reach it: he returned home in a military uniform. The whole rail network was put on a military footing. New railway lines had to be constructed in a hurry to serve the front. From our family Mother's brother fought at the front and her sister was an army doctor.

What did my parents give me? What did my family give? When I ask myself this, do you know what I think of involuntarily? That my parents and all those people who have borne the tragic burden of these years of our history, who have borne on their shoulders that heavy load, did not have an opportunity to realize themselves as they would have wished. That is probably why they made it their aim in life at least to achieve through their children those precious things which were quite out of reach for the overwhelming majority of them. As you know, we Russians have the expression 'to lift children'. It is in my view a very instructive metaphor. But I would even say this: our parents did not give us only an education. By the way they lived their lives they developed in us a sense of responsibility – for our deeds and our behaviour. And perhaps the most important thing that my parents gave me was a capacity to share other people's needs and to enter into their grief, their pain: the quality of empathy . . . No, not a single generation lives in vain on this sinful earth.

These pictures of my childhood lack completeness, they seem to be very sketchy. One of the reasons, perhaps, is the endless 'moves' we endured.

As a result of our frequent changes of abode I had to change schools many times. And that, of course, created certain difficulties. Each move meant new teachers, a different level of instruction, different demands and different schoolmates. And in general increased interest in the new girl that was inevitable in such cases.

Always the new girl? But does it not seem to you that this has followed you in your adult life? For about two years I have been accompanying you and Mikhail Sergeyevich on official trips and I see how people's interest and journalistic curiosity in you has gradually increased. Not only in the President — that's normal — but in you too. When, during the campaign before the Party Congress, he visited the Second Moscow watch factory, I heard the women in their white coats, the ones who assemble the watches and who had crowded into the workshop, asking as they craned their necks: 'Has Raisa come? Where is she?' You will forgive me for quoting them literally, without your patronymic. After all, as a woman acquires fame in Russia the first thing she loses is her patronymic.

And what then?

I told them No, Raisa Maksimovna had not come along — it was a meeting to deal with strictly Party matters.

And what did they say?

They were disappointed.

Really? Well, the inevitable curiosity and a certain lack of trust in a new girl had an effect, of course, both on my studies and on how I felt. Throughout the years of childhood and youth I have experienced a sort of internal constraint, a feeling of diffidence, sometimes of isolation. After all, children have very odd ways.

Have you fully overcome that diffidence?

I don't know, any more than I know whether it ought to be 'fully' overcome. But the situation of being 'always the new girl' led me at the same time to develop contact with people. I simply had to become more social.

The school of my childhood was not the modern school with all its equipment and furniture. It was completely different. I repeat, the schools varied in a way but were in the most important respects identical. Crudely knocked-together desks, home-made alphabet books, and during the war home-made exercise books, mostly made out of poor-quality paper. And even home-made ink.

Home-made ink?

Yes — made from soot. There was one text-book to every four or five pupils. During the war a daily bowl of watery soup for lunch. I can remember all of us children at that time, dressed in jerseys, padded jackets or at best in coats and an 'overcoat' out of some homespun or cotton material. There was such material, known as 'serge'. I received my first real overcoat as a present from my mother and father when I was already a university student. It had a small fur collar — a 'Boston', according to my mother. I wore it for a long time. The whole family remembers that coat. My father won a thousand roubles in a draw, and my mother says friends helped them to buy the coat in the village store. Such things were in short supply! Everybody remembers the coat — it really was a milestone in the family history. You know, we all turned up at the university in what we had — one person in her mother's overcoat, another in someone's jacket. That's the way it was.

My mother Aleksandra Petrovna

My father Maksim Andreyevich, who died in 1986

My first school and my class

My brother Yevgeni, 1953

My younger sister 'Lyudochka'

The year I finished school, 1949

In the last year at Moscow University

With children of teachers and staff of the university at Stromynka during my student years. In the centre is my best friend Nina Lyakisheva. How young we were!

In the faculty of philosophy at the Stavropol agricultural institute, where I used to teach

A student at Moscow University, 1953

All the same, it was my school, and, like my childhood, it remains dear to me. I was fond of the teachers. My girl friends. We sang in the school choir. We produced plays on a stage in the school. The teachers and the head of the school took part in the plays along with us. Such things are now almost impossible, or perhaps that's how it seems to me.

At gymnastics we used to construct a human pyramid. I was always lifted up to the very top, probably because I was the lightest. We went on marches. We collected scrap metal and waste paper, planted out the school yard and published a wall newspaper. We organized school parties. We danced. And we received our first love letters.

What else remains in my mind about my school years? We used to help the families who had lost members in the war. We made solemn vows to each other – to be faithful, always to stick together, to help each other and never to conceal anything from each other. We sealed our vows with 'Pioneer's Honour' or 'Komsomol's honour'. And we even mixed drops of our blood by making cuts in our fingers. I remember that too.

My father and mother did not go to school. In fact I never called them 'father and mother'. It was 'Mama and Papa'. Neither did I use 'Batyushka and Matushka' – it was not done. Just Papa and Mama. And we always addressed them as 'You' – in the second person plural. I can't recall an instance when my parents were summoned to the school. And they never checked on my homework. Only sometimes my father would tell me how he was educated. He was an educated man. He told me about the period of 'school reforms', when pupils moved from class to class according to the votes they received. The 'results' of the ballot were confirmed by the teachers at class meetings. It was up to the children whether they did their exercises or not. 'And look at an impressive product of that system,' my father would conclude, pointing at himself with a grin.

*Leaving it to the children to decide . . . Today, at any rate in
my home, it would be dangerous even to mention such a thing.*

I completed the tenth grade in the town of Sterlitamak in
Bashkiria. My school-leaving certificate said that I was
'awarded a gold medal for excellent results and exemplary
conduct'. That gave me, and I quote from the certificate, 'the
right to enter institutes of higher education in the USSR
without entry examination'. That was the second year that
gold medals were awarded. I chose to enter the 'Lomonosov'
State University in Moscow.

What year was that?

It was 1949. I was seventeen.
Like many others, I also realized in childhood the importance of books, that miracle of miracles created by humanity.
Books, the great works of literature, were my constant need
and love in those years. I was not alone, as I have said, in
experiencing this. It was precisely in those years that our
country became, as we say today, 'a country of readers'. True,
there weren't very many books to be had. No great choice.
But we read everything that came our way, everything we
could lay our hands on. And every book was a revelation to
us.
The happiest and brightest pages of my childhood that now
float into my memory are of reading books in the family circle.
I loved to read aloud. What wonderful evenings they were!
The wood would be crackling in the fireplace or the stove.
Mama would be cooking supper. My brother and younger
sister would snuggle up to me side by side. And I would read.
My father was seldom with us, very seldom. In those days you
know how people worked – without any days off and without
holidays. I remember that my father was 'compensated' for his
holiday. That was the expression – 'compensation for holiday
not taken'. He never went on holiday, but simply received

additional pay and went on working the whole year round. And so it went on, year after year.

We read everything: Panferov's *Bruski*, Sholokhov's *Quiet Flows the Don*, Tolstoy's *Anna Karenina*, Victor Hugo's *Notre Dame*, Dreiser's *An American Tragedy*, Dumas's *The Three Musketeers*, and his *Count of Monte Cristo*. We read Gogol – *Evenings on a Farm near Dikanka*, Boris Polevoi's *The Story of a Real Man*, Fadeyev's *The Young Guard*, and Simonov's poetry. And when my father was with us I always read Taras Shevchenko, above all his *Thoughts*. For example:

My thoughts, my thoughts, what pain you bring!
Why do you rise up at me in such gloomy rows? . . .

Or, again:

It is hard, very hard, for a lonely orphan.
Bitter yearning and sorrow could make me jump from
    the bridge
To drown and end this wandering from place to place.
Life is unkind, unwelcoming, and I have nowhere to
    hide . . .

And, again:

What use to me are my dark brows and brown eyes?
Or my maidenly chastity that passes so swiftly.
My youth is being wasted for nothing
And my dark brows bleached by the wind . . .

We were very fond of *Katerina* and *The Wide Dnepr*. I have been reading to you in Russian, but my father liked those poems to be read to him in the original Ukrainian – it sounds quite different!

The edition of The Kobza-player *that she holds in her lap is in*

*some way like a Bible – a very important, beautifully bound volume.
She easily finds her way through it. Nevertheless she has some difficulty
switching between the Russian to the Ukrainian: it happens quite
often with people who like to listen to Ukrainian and even sing
Ukrainian songs. I, for example, cannot say Ukrainian lyrics, I just
can't get the pronunciation right.*

Whenever I pick up a volume of Shevchenko I immediately
think of my father. I thought of him when I was last in the
Ukraine. I had a meeting with some writers in the republic,
and we talked about Shevchenko and his *Kobza-player*. My
father was so fond of it!

My brother is three years younger than I, and my sister is
six years younger. Each of us has, naturally, chosen his or her
own way in life, his own career and fate. I always regarded
my sister as a child who I, as the older one, took care of.
Even today I still call her by the diminutive 'Lyudochka'.
When I left home to study in Moscow my sister was only
eleven. Of the childhood incidents connected with her and
which I recall most often I would like to mention two.
She, my brother and I were playing a game we were very
fond of: guessing names that each of us had thought of,
male or female. It was her turn to think up a name. For
a long time we just couldn't guess what it was. No matter
how we tried it was to no avail. It even came to tears. We
began to suspect her of cheating us. Then my mother
intervened. Finally my sister revealed the name to us. She
said it was a man's name – 'Byvalocha'.

We burst out laughing, and understood at once who it
referred to. At that time, as you know, there were no hotels
in the smaller towns and villages. Travellers stayed with
friends, and one of my father's colleagues was a frequent visitor
in my parents' house. He was a good story-teller, a man who
had been around a lot, and all our family loved to listen to
him in the evenings. He always started every story with the

words 'And so, *byvalocha*,* we . . .' The whole family made
fun of his use of the word. But for my little sister it became
a proper name, and that was what she had chosen. I can't
remember now what the man's proper name was. But I remember very well his invariable *byvalocha*. Actually my brother and
I spent a couple of days trying to puzzle it out. Then came
the time for tears and mutual accusations, until finally she
admitted that the name she had thought of was 'Byvalocha'.

*That is a game that relies on mutual honesty – we used to have
something like it in our family.*

Yes, children's games are all based on playing fair. And
here's a second incident. German prisoners-of-war were
brought into railway construction during the war. A fire broke
out in the place where we were then living and several houses
were burnt to the ground. Others were partly damaged and
needed repair. Among the latter was the house that our family
was occupying. The Germans mended the roof of our house
and helped us in other ways. My sister – she was very small,
with blue eyes and fair hair – continually attracted their attention. On one occasion as I was playing in the courtyard I saw
a German go up to my sister and stretch out a hand to stroke
her head. My heart shrank from fear. In a flash I was at her
side and dragged her close to me. Only then did I look at the
German, and I suddenly realized that he was crying. You
know, I was really shaken! And there we stood – the young
German weeping, with his head hung low, and I, a young
girl, and my young sister clutching me in fright.

When I recall that scene today I think again and again about
those feelings that then possessed me and all of us in those
frightful days of the German invasion, and I think of the
monstrous tragedy that befell millions of totally innocent
people.

* In Russian, *byvalocha* means once upon a time.

And I now recall seeing you at the cemetery for Soviet prisoners-of-war in Stukenbrock in West Germany.

Yes, I had very mixed feelings when, along with a number of public figures accompanying Mikhail Sergeyevich on his official visit to West Germany, we went to pay our respects at the graves of our unfortunate compatriots. A great number of Germans also arrived at the cemetery on that day. And it seemed to me that the spirit of reconciliation had descended upon that sorrowful place called Stukenbrock for the benefit of all of us, the living and the dead. Forgiveness. You cannot live hating all the time. I believe that those endless rows of graves – not only in Stukenbrock but in our country too – summon us ultimately not to revenge but to reason . . .

My sister graduated from a medical school. She is a doctor. Her husband is an engineer. She already has a grown-up son and a little granddaughter.

And your brother?

His life worked out differently. He is a gifted and talented person. But his potentialities were not fated to be realized. His talents turned out to be unwanted and were ruined. My brother drinks and spends many months in hospital. His fate is a tragedy for Mother and Father. For me it is a constant source of pain which I have carried in my heart for more than thirty years now. His tragedy brought me a lot of sorrow, all the more so since we were very close in our childhood: we were always very sincerely attached to one another. It is very hard and painful.

Raisa Maksimovna withdrew into herself. And I began to think again about Mother Russia and drink: there are too many very similar, purely Russian disasters in the history of practically every family in the country, irrespective of its position in society. Even today our families are plagued by the same Russian curse.

The time had come to ask a leading question about some other subject. But I just couldn't think of a question. I myself have things to recall on this theme that we touched on by chance.

As I looked back on one or the other period of my life I discovered unexpectedly something surprising! [*My host resumed our conversation without any leading questions.*] Perhaps not so much surprising as natural. All my memories of my childhood, adolescence, youth and even adult years are in my case invariably accompanied by some colourful and powerful impression derived from Nature. I am convinced that this springs from my childhood. I grew up in the midst of Nature. Nature and children constitute in my view a sort of single source.

The pure beauty of the natural world has nothing to rival it in this world. I always carry with me the smell of the cherry tree and of pine needles. The joy of hearing the noise of the streams in the Urals in the spring. In the Stavropol region spring passes very quickly; there are no streams; they are in the Urals. It is a real joy. The joy of streams rushing down in the spring and the deep snowdrifts on a frosty, sunny day. And the beauty of the emerald-coloured moss and the patterned embroidery on it – cloudberries, whortleberries, columbines. And all the different kinds of mushrooms hiding themselves away – milk-caps and milk agaric, boletus and Russula. It all belongs back there, to my childhood. And it is from there, I believe, out of my childhood, that springs – for me too – that nostalgia for the silver birch or a field of rye or wheat, edged with cornflowers and camomile, that lives eternally in every Russian's heart. Then later comes the yearning for the scarlet Stavropol steppe in springtime, ablaze with tulips to the horizon. And for the crimsons and violets and greens and yellows of autumn in the North Caucasus.

I am convinced that the maltreatment of the natural world and its impoverishment leads to the impoverishment of the

human soul. It is related to the outburst of violence in human
society. To save the natural world today means to save what
is human in humanity.

In an interview he once gave Mikhail Sergeyevich was asked
what was his favourite leisure occupation and he replied: walking on forest paths. Yes, the tracks in the Moscow region, in
the Stavropol steppe, the foothills of the Great Caucasus range
– he has covered hundreds of kilometres along them. They
have provided mental balance, faith and strength.

Among Mikhail Sergeyevich's favourite songs are: 'When I
go walking near Moscow, Where the grass smells of mint,
Nature whispers to me lovingly Her secret words . . .' Then
there's 'The Russian Field' – 'The field, the Russian field, The
moon shines down or the snow falls, In joy and pain we are
together, I shall never forget.' He is very fond of those songs
and he often sings them.

You know [*she often begins a new idea with these words – 'you
know' – as though she were testing a little bridge before venturing on
to it*] the philosopher Georg Wilhelm Friedrich Hegel wrote
that philosophy is an epoch grasped in thought . . . What an
amazing definition! But what is a song? It is also an epoch,
the fate of a nation or of a man. Only it is 'grasped' in music,
in a melody and in a word, but ultimately in feeling. The
songs of my childhood were: 'Kakhovka, Kakhovka, my very
own rifle . . .' 'The order's given – he to the West, she to the
East . . .', 'The apple and pear trees were in blossom, Mist
floated over the river . . .', 'Dark night, Only bullets whistle
over the steppe, Only the wind hums in the wires, Dimly
twinkle the stars . . .', 'The steppe all around, A long road
ahead, In that remote steppe, A coachman was dying . . .' So
very moving in its 'Russian-ness', the death of that unknown
coachman has now lasted longer than any human life, more
than a century. 'There is a cliff on the Volga, overgrown with
moss from top to bottom . . .', 'The fire burns briskly in the
stove, The sap drops on the logs like tears, And in the dug-out

the harmonica sings to me of your smile and your eyes . . .',
'Arise, vast country! Into battle to the death! With the savage
Fascist force, with the cursed horde . . .'

A song that came later but found a way to our hearts, 'This
Victory Day still smells of gunpowder, It's a celebration with
greying hair, It is happiness with tears in your eyes . . .' Yes,
although it came a good deal later, it also became inseparable
from the songs of my generation.

They say the heart sees better than anything. Tell me, whose
heart, having lived through all that and having taken it in,
will not respond to human grief and human goodness?

The voices of Ruslanova, Utesov, Shulzhenko, Bernes,
Kozlovsky, Lemeshev – how we came to love their gramophone
records! And for how many years have I, like so many others
of my generation, preserved those records so carefully. In the
same way as I preserve in my memory the inexpressibly sad,
although not always sober, voices of the blind and the invalids
of the war and post-war years – in the bazaars, in the crowds,
the railway stations and in the carriages of the mainline and
local trains. Voices singing, not boldly but rather sadly, about
battles and attacks, death and love. The war is over, but its
sad, heart-breaking melody has long been floating around us,
like smoke from a passing train. People were singing everywhere, in the trains, in the parks, outside houses, and we the
children were the most faithful listeners.

Last year, accompanying Mikhail Sergeyevich on a trip, I
spent some time in the Sverdlovsk region. It is the region of
the semi-precious stones of the Urals, malachite and rock
crystal, and magnificent, severe but at the same time wonderful natural surroundings. It is the country of Bazhov, the
author of remarkable stories about the Urals, and of Mamin-
Sibiryak, author of *Privalov's Millions*. Then the 'holy place of
the Urals' – the town of Verkhoturye, founded in the sixteenth
century, through which trade between Europe and Siberia took
place along the River Tura. It is a town with unique monu-

ments of the past — a fortress, churches and monasteries.

There were a great many railways built in the Urals in the war years, and my father was one of those who worked on them. Our family had to move along as the new railroads were built. We travelled as best we could: in railway freight wagons, on trolleys on the temporary railroad, or on sleighs across the trackless *taiga*. I have particularly vivid memories of the latter. The *taiga* in winter. A really hard frost. Miles from anywhere. We children in the sleighs, wrapped up in sheepskin coats, the horses sinking up to their stomachs in the snow, snowflakes falling from the shaggy branches of the fir-trees and cedars. And occasionally, from above, a penetrating, blinding ray of sunshine. Our stops, to spend the night or to rest, in the God-forsaken villages or huts we found along the way, quite cut off from the world. You have to bear in mind that in those war years the *taiga* was a dangerous place to be, not only in itself, but also because it served as a refuge for all kinds of escaped criminals, deserters and even prisoners of war on the run.

It was to the Urals that equipment was evacuated from industrial centres, factories and workshops in the western Soviet Union. And machinery and weapons were transported from the Urals to the front. I spent a considerable part of my 'Urals' childhood in the Sverdlovsk district. It was there, in the old church that had been turned into a club, that I saw the film *Chapayev* on innumerable occasions. It was there that we played our girlish games and teased each other. And it was there, in the town of Alapayevsk, that I went to the theatre for the first time in my life. I saw the play *Platon Krechet* — I remember that too.

Even now you are involved in the world of children. I have in mind your charitable activities.

Yes, we were all children once. Unfortunately, we often forget it. What can be more precious than children's health —

physical, moral and intellectual. I think of Armenia and those tragic days following the earthquake. I shall never forget the pitiful ruins where a family house had stood. The faces of the people . . . The shouts and groans. The shock the people suffered. And the tears. Thousands of people's thoughts and hopes and dreams buried in a moment. Tens and hundreds of tiny coffins just standing on the street. I visited the hospitals where the injured children were being treated. Do you know how I was greeted by a boy whose legs had been crushed – the school had collapsed in the middle of a lesson! 'Auntie Raya, Auntie Raya! I shall never go to school again!' he shouted from his bed almost before I entered the ward.

What could I say to him? How could I console him? Whatever happens to our children – even if it is an act of blind fate – we adults look into children's eyes at such times not only with sympathy but also with a feeling of guilt as well.

All the same – what did you tell him?

I begged him to be strong. 'You are a man,' I said. 'And your mother is beside you.' I said we would build new schools in his town, beautiful and strong, in which there would be no need to be frightened. I held him by the hand and he gradually calmed down.

Nowadays no one is surprised at someone's performing acts of charity, and certainly not an American reader. And I would not wish to give an account of my 'good deeds'. I only want to say that concern for children and charity work in that field is today in our society not a matter of passing fancy or of fashion but the most pressing necessity. I did not hesitate in making my choice about where to direct my efforts. I had no difficulty in deciding upon the field of children's welfare. I am a patron of the Central Republican hospital for children in Moscow which treats children from practically all our republics. Mikhail Sergeyevich hands over the fees and other awards he receives, including his Nobel Prize, mainly for the needs

of the health service. He often entrusts me with the task of
handing over the money or medical equipment. In this field
he has done a great deal for the medical institutions in various
parts of the country – in Byelorussia, the Ukraine, Uzbekistan,
Kazakhstan – and including the hospital in the Red Guard
district of Stavropol where he was born.

The hospital of which I am a patron has also received
through my husband a good deal of modern foreign equipment
and help with hard currency. The doctors, mainly quite young
people and fanatics for their work, have had the possibility of
working in the best clinics in the United States and Germany.
The Soviet Union is now receiving substantial humanitarian
assistance from various countries. I want especially to thank
future American readers. A considerable part of that assistance,
some of it addressed to me, comes from the United States.
The readiness of the American people to respond to our needs
evokes a warm feeling of gratitude in Soviet people and in me
personally.

I visited Chernobyl along with my husband. I came across
many children whose lives were shaken by that disaster. I
visited the offices of the association 'Haematologists of the
World – For the Children', the aim of which is to treat children
suffering from leukaemia, and I also visited the headquarters
of the fund set up by the Japanese businessman Sasakavi called
'Aid for the Children of Chernobyl'. Quite recently I paid one
of my regular visits to the radiological department of the
hospital, where I met and chatted with the patients, with
those under observation by the hospital, and even with their
families.

There is something with which I can never reconcile myself
– and that is the feeling that people are doomed. I have already
told you about the Republican children's hospital. The children who are the most seriously ill are sent there from the
whole of Russia, actually from the whole of the USSR. Alas,
there are among them some who are incurable. I went along

with a crowd of children to see their common playroom. It was also full of children. There prevailed a sort of suppressed, rather tentative noise. You know how children play when they are very sick. And in among that crowd of children – and there were children in the hospital from practically all our nationalities – there was a young woman sitting on a low chair, clutching to herself a three-year-old boy while she stared motionless ahead. When she suddenly caught sight of me she said in a muffled, tired voice without any hysteria, at the extreme limit of human strength of which only a woman's, a mother's heart is capable: 'Raisa Maksimovna, help us! Do something! We came to Moscow seven times and only at the seventh time did we succeed in getting a place in this hospital, in the haematological department. But they simply examined us and said: "Go back home, there is no hope for the boy." Help us!'

I felt unsteady on my legs. I took the little boy from his mother, stroked his head and exchanged glances with the mother, after which words have no meaning.

Later, in the chief doctor's office, the doctors tried to convince me that it made more sense to send the boy home: he was practically doomed. If he were to have an operation, which he was unlikely to survive, there was only one chance in a hundred that he would live. 'But there is that one chance, and who knows, he . . .' I begged them to do everything possible and even more. 'I beg you,' I said.

The boy's name was Dima. I learned yesterday that there had been no miracle. He had died.

When I departed that evening I took a bundle of letters with me in my briefcase. Later, at home, I spent a long time studying them. The letters already bore evidence of having been sorted: they had little pieces of paper pinned to their corners with handwritten notes on them, saying who they were from and when received. Some of them were distinguished by having cardboard folders with official abbreviations on them. I looked at the envelopes and then understood how the selection had been made — the letters with a cardboard cover were the ones that had been addressed to 'Mrs Gorbachev, The Kremlin, Moscow'. Those with an even shorter address — 'Gorbachev, R.M., Moscow' — they had no folder, but just a scrap of paper indicating from whom the letter came and when. A real office at home.

More than in any other country it is the custom in Russia to address letters to the top people. This epistolary link between the people and the centre of power is completely in accord with our national tradition. The same is true of the habit of assuming that the big bosses are accommodated exclusively in the Kremlin although there has not been a single apartment there for ages, with the exception of Lenin's and that is no longer lived in.

The wives of our biggest leaders have not, I believe, been written to for several decades, though I may be wrong.

There are so many letters that she now needs an office to process them. But she apparently does not have one yet: the scraps of paper were signed in the very same familiar writing. There was no indication of the assistant who should have handled the documents. There was just a gap.

What are these letters about? They are asking for some request to be carried out. In Russia that kind of letter must of course contain requests, more requests and still more requests, dictated most often not by a passing fancy but by the imperfections in our society and by hopes placed in the 'top' people. That's what the letter writers expect from the people they write to.

These letters turned out to be all connected in some way with children. The boys and girls of the Kemerovo musical school express their thanks for being received in Moscow during their concert tour in the capital. Thanks again for two 'Yasnaya Polyana' accordions made specially for the 'New Names' programme of the Soviet cultural fund by the Tula 'Melodiya' association and handed over to the school as a gift. A long, rambling letter in a very elevated tone from the actor and director Rolan Bykov about the needs of the children's film centre in Moscow. A little blue, patterned and even, it seemed, scented envelope slipped out of the bulky bundle reminding one of the Smolny Institute with its genteel archaic manner. Natalia Sats: 'I hope to see you in the middle of May and to tell you about my project for organizing an association called "Art to the Children".' The sheet of paper the letter was written on was also very fancy, blue and crisp like starched material.

There were some letters written in a firm, strong hand on thick sheets of paper at the top of which was printed in Russian and English: 'Bekhtereva, Natalia Petrovna, Member of the Academy of Science of the USSR, Director of the Institute for Experimental Medicine, Head of the Department of the Neurophysiology of Man, etc.' In short, one of the most 'titled' women in the USSR.

'At last, quite recently, we managed, after overcoming an endless series of obstacles, to conclude a contract with a Swedish firm for the supply of a positron-emitting tomograph which for me will always be associated with you — thank you for your help. We are doing everything to realize the possibilities that are opening up and to produce our own analogues as quickly as possible . . .' And further: 'From what I know of the mechanisms of the brain our society is now passing through a phase which alone will enabled it to achieve a new level socio-politically and economically . . .'

In every one of her letters there is at least a line about the long-expected tomograph — how it 'feels' and how it is working for the benefit of the Soviet health service. Then, at the end: 'I think about you, but now for some reason, when you look so well on the screen and you are received so warmly everywhere, I worry about you . . .' The language is clear and Russian, and the handwriting also looks as if it were printed. When my hostess handed these letters over to me for a time she said in a sad tone: 'Natalia Petrovna has suffered a tragedy. Her son and her husband died almost simultaneously.'

Concerning the hospitalization in West Germany of the boy V. Uvarov. Because of the impossibility of providing in the USSR the treatment for the disease of the blood diagnosed in the boy, his parents sent a letter to Mikhail and Raisa Gorbachev asking for help in organizing treatment in the German Federal Republic where the necessary methods of treatment and medicines are available. Reacting to this letter, Mikhail Gorbachev approached Helmut Kohl with a request to help the boy. The request was well received. Today V. V. Tyutyunov, Councillor at the Soviet Embassy in West Germany, reported that Valeri Uvarov has been admitted to the children's clinic in Hanover. Treatment is being directed by Professor Hubert Polivoda. The treatment is being administered by Professor Hans-Jurg Rum. The cost of the boy's and his mother's stay is being borne by the charitable organization 'Care Deutschland'.

V. Aleksandrov, Assistant to the Secretary of the Central Committee of the Communist Party of the Soviet Union.

Since our last meeting at the Republican hospital a lot of things have changed for the better. Professor E. B. Vladimirsky and I have organized a new institute based on the hospital as well as two departments in the city to cope with Muscovites suffering from diseases of the blood; we are carrying out repairs in two departments on the floor where you inspected the blood bank. With help from German colleagues and the firm of Stig we have started to organize in one of the departments the first children's department for transplanting bone marrow.

Yours – Professor A. G. Rumyantsev.

It seemed to me there was some connection between those two letters.

A young boy, Ilyusha Malyshev, sends thanks for the guitar he was presented with and for the help given to his mother, his little brother and himself to obtain a long-awaited apartment. 'Raisa Maksimovna! In the summer I gave paid concerts in offices and factories. Along with your wonderful guitar we earned 340 roubles which we donated to the charitable project Samantha . . . They listen to "my" wartime songs and they go so well that people even cry . . .'

Oh, I know that boy. Both the boy and his mother. I was present when R. M. Gorbachev met them at the Culture Fund. As I understood it, the letter was written a long time ago, because the boy is now studying at the music school attached to the Conservatory. At the meeting he was giving a kind of 'report' about his creative work in the last two years. But I was moved not only by the boy, so slim and romantic, with an impressive head of hair and delicate, nervous fingers. I was touched by the simplicity and dignity with which the two women conducted themselves — Raisa Gorbachev and Ilyusha's mother, Nina Davydovna. There was no hint of the 'benefactress' and the 'petitioner'. The two women chatted together calmly and sensibly, and not only about the gifted lad and his immediate future. To a much greater extent they talked about the life which was seething outside the house on the Gogol Boulevard where the Soviet Culture Fund was located.

Dear Raisa [*Signora Fanfani begins her letter, written in Italian*],

I am very sorry not to have been able to see you, at least to shake your hand and wish you happiness in the New Year. On behalf of Amintore I send the President the warmest and most sincere wishes for success in his work for the good of the Russian people. Baron von Thyssen, whom I met in Rome, sends you greetings and good wishes.

I am sending you a list of the help which we have produced for your hospitals from October to the present day. I am happy to have been able, without help from the Government or the ministries, to carry out this voluntary mission and to have collected, prepared and despatched it all with my own hands. We have done it all with the best of will and in the hope that the Soviet Union will not need help in the near future. Then we shall visit Moscow only to become acquainted with its culture. In any case I would like you to know that you have a friend in Italy, a real friend who loves the Russian people and loves the Gorbachev family.

Dear Raisa Maksimovna!

From now on I have the right to address you in that way, because there is nothing dearer to me than your name. I shall always, to the very end of my days, be grateful to you and Mikhail Sergeyevich. Despite being so busy you found the time to help my son to overcome a most serious illness. I have already visited him twice in the clinic (the Burdenko hospital) and I am able to tell you that the danger of death has passed. Although his condition is still very serious and requires long and major treatment, the worst is behind us. According to what the doctors have told me, this is the first case in the world to date where a person with such an illness has survived.

How grateful I am to you for your goodness and kindness!

My son had a purulent abscess in the brain with the discharge of pus into the ventricles of the brain. The skilful hands of the doctors and your kind response to me in my grief performed a miracle.

Four years ago my wife died while undergoing an operation. She was my best friend, my comrade and a person very dear to me. Now I have trouble with my son. My great grief prompted me to write to you with a request for help, and you and your husband helped me. I don't intend to write to the newspapers or make big speeches. I will tell you only one thing. Remember that there is in this country a man ready to give his all for you, even his life.

I am a former airman and now a reserve officer. I have two sons, both of them officers, and one of them suffered a great misfortune. What you did for me and my son cannot be expressed in everyday language. To the end of my days I shall remember your goodness and kindness.

Perhaps my letter will seem to you rather disjointed. But believe me when I say that these words come from the very depths of a father's heart. Again and again I thank you and your husband for your kindness and sympathy. Not every person would be capable of carrying such a burden on his shoulders like the one you and your husband bear, and still find time to share the misfortune that has struck another person. But that's what you did.

Greetings and unlimited gratitude! I am already 66 and have been around a lot, but such human compassion I have never met before. I wish you and Mikhail Sergeyevich the very best of health, joy and happiness and everything of the best. Once again – a huge fatherly and human thank you. With sincere respect and gratitude,

Sudakov, Vladimir Dmitrievich.

I decided to quote this letter in its entirety. It was night-time when I read it, and beyond the dark I could see the man, the father, who had written it. There is plenty of grief in our country, but few, too few, instances of its being overcome. In this sense the letter struck me as being a rare human document. Let it fly away and scatter a glimmer of hope to all of us sufferers – in Russia, in America, wherever you like.

Among the letters was a sheet of paper bearing a translation of a letter from Yoko Ono, widow of the legendary John Lennon. She wrote about the good impressions she had at a meeting of the international forum in Moscow, and suggested they should write a 'women's' book together.

And then another envelope, without any scraps of paper attached, fell out of the bundle. It had also been opened and I automatically

took the letter out of it . . . 'Dear Rayechka, greetings . . .'

It was something rather unusual. More even than Signora Fan-fani's manner. I read the first line again, and no, I had not made a mistake. 'Dear Rayechka, greetings . . .' I then realized that the letter must have got stuck to others and had landed in my bundle by chance. I folded it up and put it back into the envelope. On the back of the envelope was the name: Alferova, L. Her sister? A relation? A friend?

In a school photograph that I was shown that evening they are sitting there, the children of the forties, bunched around their teacher. They squeeze up to each other with a look of curiosity and something more . . . They cling to each other because like that it is warmer and safer in that insecure world.

It is probably the same in this world today. It is a difficult business – in all ages – to be at the very centre, the focus of other people's hopes. To be the last resort for someone's desperate entreaties and sacred and so very just demands. Not a single man in the world (perhaps with the exception of the one and only, and he doesn't yet live in the Kremlin) is in a position to carry out everything that is expected of him.

In that photo I recognized Raisa Gorbachev by one single feature. By the same one that brought her to the very top of the very risky gymnastic pyramids at school in the 1940s.

Look in the photo for the slimmest and smallest girl. That is Raisa.

CHAPTER THREE

University Years

I am on my way again to the President's suburban residence. It appears that winter has returned at last to Moscow, having been driven away by some natural or manmade disaster. It is a good sign. The surrounding forests are submerged in it. Even along the Rublyov highway, which Muscovites still call in the old way a 'government' highway, the snowdrifts mount up to the very windows of the car.

The highway is fairly well maintained and regularly repaired, but, frankly speaking, it is becoming less 'governmental' every year. The road is being democratized before our very eyes. I drove along it for the first time in 1984. Then it still existed in a state of mysterious, aristocratic estrangement from the other ordinary roads and footpaths in the Moscow region. A person driving under the arch made by the overhanging fir-trees had a feeling of pride: he was driving along the road of official success.

I recall how, as a casual passer-by, I was struck by the strict enforcement and the hierarchical perfection of the prevailing regulations: our Volga was forced several times, not just to move to one side, but to dig its nose right into the snow and freeze, as small insects freeze at the sight of danger, and so free the road for the benefit of the grim-looking bullet-proof ZILs — the earthly means of transport of the Soviet gods — overtaking us or rushing towards us. It was in the direction of Rublyov that, for God knows how long, the country houses of the Soviet elite were situated. The regime operating on the Rublyov highway was an exact parallel of the regime of the rulers of the day.

Some time in 1986 I began travelling by that road more or less regularly. I would not say that it happened immediately, but it was very noticeable that practically in front of my eyes the well-manned traffic police posts disappeared: several of their little sentry-boxes are now simply empty, leading me to think of the demilitarization of the very regime. Certain sacred rights vanished – the road became a road again and not an exclusive 'highway'. The average citizen with a little cottage in the country loads down his little Zaporozhets with long-sought-after building material and scurries along, like a fish in shallow water, along the road which at one time he didn't dare to put a foot on. Then cars with foreign registration plates appeared on the road – too many, perhaps – because, as they say, all kinds of foreign enterprises began eagerly to buy up plots of land and buildings in that very Russian countryside for out-of-town offices.

What is more, the number of ZIL limousines dropped sharply, as in Moscow as a whole: in the period of perestroika not only was Soviet officialdom reduced in numbers, it also switched from the huge, period automobiles to more modest and economic ones which were also less noticeable in the life of the capital. It is sufficient to say that even the Politburo switched to using Volgas. One could not have imagined such a thing happening in 1984.

No longer do drivers get pushed into the ditch by the all-powerful striped police baton (no face to be seen, just a baton sticking out from the window of the follow-up car as the very embodiment of authority). I saw the President's car several times on that road. What is more I could even distinguish his features – he was sitting on the front seat for some reason and reading a paper. It seems that even the ZILs have become more transparent in the time of glasnost.

I cannot say that there has been greater order on the Rublyovka in recent years, but there has certainly been an improvement in the way people are treated.

The road is very winding. They say that those frequent bends were introduced in the 1930s so that potential evildoers should not be able to take aim. The car went smoothly after the heavy snowfalls, giving the impression of moving rather like a sleigh, not a machine, not something mechanical. All the same the journey took ten or fifteen minutes longer than on the previous day.

But, you know, there is nowhere better for thinking than on a journey. Especially on a road that reminds you so well of the sleigh tracks of old, a road that goes through the snow-covered plains of central Russia that prompt unhurried thoughts.

I was thinking that, after all, the nature of a regime changes under the influence of the character, and not just the character, but simply the appearance of a woman whose book you Western readers are now holding in your hands.

Why? The fact of her appearing just once alongside the powers that be in 1985 made those powers more attractive, more accessible and even happier. And younger looking too, which is also not unimportant if you bear in mind the fact that in recent years the personification of power took the form of feeble old age alienated from reality.

Krasnoyarsk, Norilsk, Donetsk . . . A kindergarten, a nursery school, a children's home . . . The appearance, among the usual collection of male official faces, of a woman's face, is attractive because it is sharper and more sympathetic: both joy and sorrow are more noticeable.

That retentive memory and those observant brown eyes, developed probably in childhood, when her very way of life — practically a life on wheels — the kaleidoscope of faces, places, railway stations and country halts — forced her from her earliest years to look closely at the world coming towards her.

This time I arrived at the residence with a new toy — a Grundig tape recorder. I had had a recorder with me last time, but it was a small Japanese one, half the size of my hand. It was convenient for my conversations with Raisa Maksimovna, but it was not very convenient for Ira, the typist I had asked to transcribe the tapes. So this time I turned up with the Grundig. It was well made in the German manner, not just a Japanese toy, and, most surprising, it needed no batteries. It was plugged into the mains.

No matter how I tried, my jacket thrown off, the Grundig plug would not go into the socket above the sofa. Then I drew attention to the fact that there was one free socket next to the President's desk, one side of which was simply covered with wires. But the gap between the

*desk and the window was so narrow that I began to doubt whether
I could get through. Eighty-five kilos live weight . . . And it
wouldn't be right to move the desk: it was after all the President's
desk.*

Raisa Maksimovna caught the look of doubt on my face.

You can't make it? Let me – I can get through. Diet.

But it seems to me to be your natural shape.

Oh no [*she said, smiling*], I'm very strict with myself.

*But, thank God, I also got through. The reel on the Grundig
began to turn noiselessly.*

Georgi Vladimirovich, I understood that we were going to
talk today about the years of my youth. But even in this
section I shall find it difficult always to be saying 'my'. I shall
probably more often be saying 'we' – Mikhail Sergeyevich and
I. But nevertheless at the outset it will be 'me'. About the
years of childhood and youth and the dearest memories of that
time. Youth is, after all, just a moment, but it is the moment,
the spark that you always carry in your heart.

For me youth was above all my university years. Without
them, I tell you, there wouldn't have been any youth. That's
what I think. And I believe that without those years we would
never have become what we have become.

We would have. Only we would have been different.

I agree. I define youth as a time of poetry, of self-assertion,
of seeking for the truth and for answers to the age-old human
problems. But what was my youth distinguished by? What
was it associated with?

The first half of the 1950s. The country's post-war years. A
special period in our nation's history. Those years contained
so much: both tragic and heroic. I still find myself unable to
explain how people could do, could achieve what they did in
those unforgettable years. From where did they derive the

strength? Factories, electric power stations, towns and villages were rebuilt, and the land, devastated by war, was restored to life.

Lord! What joy we took in everything, how proud we were. Although we continued to have an unbelievably difficult life. In the collective farms the pay for a day's work was so little and so useless that they used to say: 'We work for nothing.' The most essential goods were missing from the shops and daily life. There were tremendous problems with housing . . .

Yes, a lot of things happened in those years. Testing of the atomic and later the hydrogen bomb. The end of the United States' monopoly of nuclear weapons. The Warsaw Pact. Fresh alarms for the fate of the peace that had cost us so dear. These were not abstract things, you know. It is all very important for an understanding of us and our youth.

But that's not all. There was the 'Leningrad Affair' concerning Party officials, 'The Moscow Doctors' Affair'. Those last convulsions of Stalinism were especially humiliating for a people who had been victorious and had overcome disaster at the cost of unbelievable sacrifices and suffering, and for the moral and social experience that the people had gained through the war.

Stalin died on the 5th of March 1953. We were in Moscow at the time.

What was I thinking about just now? A person's life is composed of certain external circumstances and events and his own actions and behaviour. And also of the life within himself. It is easier, of course, to reproduce the former, the external side. More difficult to reproduce the internal side. But you will agree that the sense and essence of life lies in their unity and mutual interdependence. A person's internal state, his peace, the range of the feelings possessing his spirit − it is precisely these that are often decisive in a person's taking certain decisions or performing certain acts. But identifying them is more complicated.

And so, it is 1949. I am on my way to Moscow. I am going to study.

By train?

Of course. And what a train! The carriages were over-crowded. All the seats taken, whatever ticket you had, and the luggage racks occupied too. Nowadays people put their luggage up there. But in those days people occupied the racks. What seats! People travelled standing, in the corridors and on the outside platforms. The trains crept along slowly, with long and frequent stops. Not just ours; all the trains in the country were the same. There were no sheets for the beds, and no one thought of asking for any. Instead of a buffet on the train there was only the tank of boiled water at the stations and the station markets to which everybody dashed during the stops.

And no one was afraid of missing the train.

In my view it was impossible to miss a train in those days. Even if you missed it you could catch up with it all the same. The peasants brought things to the train to sell: boiled potatoes, milk, eggs, loaves of bread, home-distilled spirits, vodka, apples and water from the well – for five kopeks a jug. Pickled cucumbers and berries. True, it was all very expensive. For the journey you had to rely mainly on what your mother had provided.

I was sad to be setting out for the first time on my own on such a long journey. The sadness of parting from my family. Parting from my school friends. Those who came to the station to see me off stood there before me. Parting from the world in which I was at home and understood. Sadness and anxiety. The beginning of the unknown, of an independent career. But at times the feeling of uncertainty and sadness would be replaced suddenly by a sense of happiness, joy and pride, the awareness that I was going to study in Moscow! Moscow, its Red Square, monuments, museums, theatres and libraries, would all be mine. I was going to study in the Moscow State University where many pillars of the country's science and culture had also studied. I was travelling in a train, but at times it seemed as if I were flying on wings.

The university – my alma mater. Mine and Mikhail Sergey-evich's. Do you know what it means literally when translated from the Latin? 'Bounteous mother.' True, with material food the universities always went short, but with spiritual food . . . Our university did indeed become for us an intellectual 'bounteous mother'. To a considerable extent it determined the development of personality and the future course of our lives.

We were part of the second post-war recruitment of students. My generation, the generation of the seventeen-year-olds, came to the university straight from school. But among those in the first recruitment were many much older people, thirty- and even thirty-five-year-olds. The 'Old Men', as we used to call them. They were those who in the war years had for various reasons interrupted their education: they had been in occupied territory, been employed somewhere, fought with the partisans, had been evacuated, or had simply not been able to obtain an education earlier. But the majority of the 'Old Men' were men who had fought at the front and been demobilized who didn't even change their military great-coats and uniform throughout their student years. They just didn't change their clothes. Both because they really had nothing special to change into and because they were in no hurry to part with their front-line youth and their front-line comradeship. This has, in my view, been depicted very well in Yuri Bondarev's *Silence* and Yuri Trifonov's *Students* and in other novels and stories of that time. Some of my age group, when they come to recall the 'Old Men', now point out first of all that they drank vodka – the front-line fighters. They did drink, of course. But those people introduced into our environment something more important. They brought a special diligence, a devotion to their work, a sense of responsibility and a realistic view of life and human relationships. They were a sort of university within the university.

The university gathered us together from the most differing corners of the country. Russians, Uzbeks, Ukrainians, Byelorussians, Kazakhs, Azerbaidjanis, Jews, Armenians, Latvians, Kirgiz, Georgians, Turkmen and more. A cross-section of the country as a whole.

There were also foreigners studying with us. Albanians, Bulgarians, Yugoslavs, Czechs . . . And they lived in the same rooms along with us. Germans, Spaniards, Koreans, Chinese, Vietnamese . . .

We were all close to each other. We studied together in the same libraries and in the same lecture-rooms. We sat our examinations, wrote our degree theses, and ate in the same canteens. We made friends and we got married. The spirit of youth and comradeship – that was the prevailing atmosphere in the university. In addition, all of us in those years were united in our optimism. Youth, the sense and awareness of our youth, comradeship and optimism. God knows where we took it from, but that's how it was. Optimism united us all. But perhaps it was simply that I perceived life like that? No, even if it is the way I perceived it, it was all the same real optimism.

How many years have flown past! And I am proud when I see, observe or hear by some echoes reaching me, that the years that have passed and sped away have not destroyed that youthful sense of fellowship and humanity in those who were then with us. They have not destroyed it.

She pauses and then repeats:

In the majority of cases it was not destroyed. At any rate in the case of those with whom I have been in contact. For example, there was Merab Mamardashvili who died recently. He studied on the same course as mine. A Georgian who became a major authority in the world of philosophy. He married a girl from my room with whom I had lived for some years. Therefore we were especially close. Merab was one of the regular visitors to our girls' quarters. There were several of them. We became accustomed to the regular visitors to our room. Merab married one of my friends and the sociologist Yuri Levada another.

Even at that time we respected Merab for his intellect. I remember how he used to help us girls to digest *Das Kapital*. I knew Merab very well. True, life later led us apart. He had a complicated career. Do you realize that, to his very last days, he tried to calm down the nationalist passions that were flaring up between the peoples? He had the courage to oppose extreme nationalism. I am proud of Merab.

Perhaps that courageous opposition to any kind of raving extremism wherever it came from, is the clearest indication of a genuine philosopher?

Perhaps. But I want to say that that was what made up our years. It was what united us. And it was what remained, in spite of any differences we may have had.

Zdenek Mlynar was on the same course as Mikhail Sergeyevich. He was also a friend of ours. As you know, he is a Czech. In 1955, to mark his graduation from the university, he presented my husband with his photograph and a copy of his thesis entitled 'The general supervision as part of the Prosecutor's work and ways of putting it into practice'. On the gift is written: 'To Mishka, a good friend, to remind him that we are lawyers with a broad profile.'

The profile did indeed turn out to be broad! He was the future ideologist of 'socialism with a human face' and, figuratively speaking, its strategist and practitioner.

We met Zdenek again in 1967. He came to Stavropol.

Mlynar was in Stavropol in 1967?

Yes, he came to visit us.

In 1967?

Yes. On the eve of all the events. And we had a meeting
with him. We met Zdenek and his wife again later, in 1990.

And there were no meetings in between?

Mikhail Sergeyevich had some meetings recently but they
were official ones. There were no private meetings. We had a
meeting in 1990. And recently Zdenek sent a letter in connection with the award of the Nobel Peace Prize to Mikhail
Sergeyevich. I will read it to you: 'Dear Misha! On this
occasion we shall probably not manage to meet. That is why
I have decided to write you a brief note. You know that I
don't like formality, but all the same I want, in my own
name and Irina's, to express our most sincere good wishes in
connection with your receiving the Nobel Peace Prize. You
have earned it and by so doing you have done more for our
common cause than could have been expected from a single
human being. Yours sincerely – Zdenek. P.S. If you need
anything from me I am always ready . . . I am worried about
a lot of things at the moment, but I know that it can't be
otherwise, and I am on the side you are on.'

  Our student days remained with us. We lived, of course,
modestly. Very modestly. In poverty, as it might appear to
someone today. The old, ancient buildings of Moscow University, in the lecture halls of which my husband and I studied,
are situated, as you know, in the centre of the city, on the
corner of Herzen Street and the Mokhovaya. The student hostel
was then located in the Sokolniki region, on the Stromynka on
the Yauza river. It was a huge, four-storey, rather forbidding
rectangular building with a large courtyard inside. The three
top floors were occupied by students and post-graduates, dis-
tributed according to their faculties – philologists, historians,
philosophers, physicists, lawyers, biologists and so forth. On

the ground floor was the library, the reading room, the student club, a hospital, a tailor's shop, the canteen and a buffet. In the corner building opposite the hostel there was a food shop. It is still there today. On the other bank of the Yauza, in the Preobrazhensky region, or, as we then called it, the 'Preobrazhenka', was a street market.

Could you make the transition to that free market?

A transition? We just crossed the bridge [*she smiled*]. It was a market for food, not for clothes.

Our Stromynka, Preobrazhenskaya Square and the Preobrazhenskaya Embankment are all, according to tradition, part of the Preobrazhenskaya *sloboda* or special district which has gone down in the history of Moscow. It was built by Peter the First. It was said that the building housing our student hostel had once served as barracks for the Petrovsky Preobrazhensky regiment. Later, in the Soviet years, two floors were built on. The nearest Metro station to the hostel is Sokolniki. It is just three stops by tram. Yes, if my memory serves me right, three. And the nearest cinema is the Rusakov club. The building, if you have ever noticed it, is of a very unusual shape, in the constructivist style.

In our first years each room in the student hostel provided accommodation for from eight to fourteen persons. It was only the students in the senior classes and post-graduates who were able to arrange themselves with four to six to a room. The furnishings were of the simplest, practically monastic; beds, a table, chairs, bedside tables, bookshelves and a wardrobe. Each floor had a communal kitchen and toilets with washbasins.

Our 'wardrobe' at that time was also very modest, if the clothes that we wore year in, year out could be dignified by the title of 'wardrobe'. There is much, very much that one might say about it.

Never mind — it's interesting.

Well, one fact at least. In the thirty-degree Moscow frosts
– and the winters were more severe then and I remember it
being even forty degrees below – we, with very few exceptions,
had no warm winter footwear, warm underwear, stockings or
winter headgear. And many of us did not have even a winter
overcoat.

We economized on everything. On food, I remember how
my friend Nina Lyakisheva's aunt tried so touchingly and in
such a motherly way to feed us. (Nina was left an orphan
during the war and was brought up in a children's home in
Tashkent.) Nina and I went down to see her in Balashikha, a
town in the Moscow region, and her aunt probably had more
than eloquent grounds for believing that we visited her mainly
for one purpose – to fortify ourselves with a little food.

We also saved money on transport. How? We simply tried
to travel without paying. Both on the trams and on the Metro.

And on the Metro?

Yes, we had a great many tricks for doing it. But I am not
going to talk about that now. My own secrets! But, no matter
how we economized, ten days before our scholarships arrived
we had no money left. As the poet Nikolai Rubtsov says: 'I
pat my pocket and it doesn't sound; I try the other – nothing
there; If I shall be famous one day, I'll take a holiday in Yalta.'
How many amazing adventures befell us for that reason! But
we always found a way out of trouble, I tell Mikhail Sergeyevich now that, whatever law they may pass, there will always
be someone who will think up a way of getting round it. We
ourselves travelled free on the trams and the Metro.

Mikhail Sergeyevich too?

Georgi Vladimirovich, you are asking provocative questions. As for the Metro, I can let you into one revealing detail:
in those days there were no automatic machines. There were
tickets. The conductors on the Sokolniki trams reluctantly

accepted our silent requests. And when of a morning the thousand-strong (I don't know exactly — there were five or six thousand of us living at the Stromynka) crowd of students filled up the tram and were jammed into it nobody asked for any tickets. Only a few conscientious conductors growled at us, but the others, the majority, paid no attention to us: they resigned themselves to the situation.

We bought the cheapest possible tickets for the theatre. They were tickets that had stamped on them: 'Top gallery, uncomfortable'. The gallery, the gallery! Whenever I enter a theatre I still look up to that gallery, because it was from there for the first time in my life that I heard an opera performed in the Bolshoi Theatre — Bizet's *Carmen* and for the first time heard a performance of Tchaikovsky's First and Sixth Symphonies. It was from the 'gods' that I saw my first ballet — Minkus's *Don Quixote*. And Chekhov's *Three Sisters* at the Moscow Arts Theatre.

And did you ever glance up at the government box, the 'Tsar's' box?

I don't think so. It didn't really interest me. As for the government box, I can tell you about another episode concerning the present day. Do you recall that that amazing tenor Luciano Pavarotti came to Moscow recently?

Yes.

Mikhail Sergeyevich and I heard him sing in the Bolshoi Theatre. One aria after another. A storm of delighted applause. I leaned across to Mikhail Sergeyevich and said: 'Surely he's not going to leave out *Ave Maria?*' 'Just wait', he said, 'be patient, he will surely sing it.' But he went on singing other things, but not *Ave* . . . Again I leaned across: 'Surely? . . .' 'Listen,' he said with a smile, 'if for some reason he doesn't sing it, so be it — I will sing *Ave Maria* for you right here.' And he added: 'True, I fear it will be my last public performance . . . Can you imagine *Ave Maria* being sung in the government box . . .'

I can't imagine it . . . Well, and did he sing it?

Who?

If the President were to sing not only Moscow would have known about it — the whole world would have known.

I have Schubert's *Ave Maria* sung by Pavarotti recorded on a record — 'Pavarotti's Greatest Hits'.

I have never heard how well the President sings, but I — and not just I — noticed long ago that he has a fine sense of humour.

Yes, he has no time for singing at the moment. And, as for his sense of humour, you are right, it is a feature of his mind. A fortunate feature. Often, in a moment, unexpectedly and in a flash, it can remove internal tension, tiredness or an awkward situation. Two examples that have suddenly come to my mind. It was during an official visit to West Germany in November last year. We were flying at night in a helicopter on the way to the airport at Frankfurt-am-Main. We were sitting in silence, weighed down by the strain of the past day. The helicopter came in to land. The people waiting for us on the ground tried to protect themselves from the gusts of wind that always accompany a helicopter's landing or take-off. Mikhail Sergeyevich then said: 'So we've combed the hair of the welcoming party. Now we can shake their hands.' And that wise-crack seemed to make everything easier, as though it had lifted from us the tiredness and burden of the whole day.

Do you remember Barcelona and the famous museum, the House of Picasso? It has a collection of the early, student works of the great artist, his ceramics, a series of variations on the theme of *The Maids of Honour* by Velazquez, which impressed Mikhail Sergeyevich and me, and a whole row of rooms entitled 'Pablo and Jacqueline'. The rooms contained nothing but portraits, paintings and sketches of his beautiful wife Jacqueline. A hundred Jacquelines look down from the walls. There were some at which Felipe, the young heir to the Spanish throne, who was accompanying us, was embarrassed to halt our large, formal procession. On one of these occasions Mikhail Sergeyevich said: 'If I were to draw Raisa Maksimovna like that she would never sleep again.' Everybody laughed.

Let us return, however, to the student years. We were 'working' students. We took jobs wherever we could. Unloading trucks of vegetables and coal at the Khimki river port and at Moscow railway stations was the sort of work our boys did. Of course, there were young people studying in our groups whose parents were 'Stalin' prize-winners, people of merit and those who were simply well provided for. Moscow society consists of many layers, like no other city in the country. Those young people did not live in the hostel. They enjoyed completely different conditions. They relaxed differently and they dressed differently. But I do not recall that I personally or those in my immediate circle felt ourselves to be reduced or deprived because of that. No. I will say more. We were happy. Happy in our youth and in our hopes for the future. Even just at being alive. That we were studying at university. That was what we valued.

Our lecturers and teachers were leading scholars. Such was the tradition. I don't know what happens now, but I hope the tradition has been preserved. The most distinguished scholars in the country were invited to lecture to us. The authors of well-known text-books, for example. Our logic lectures were given by Asmus, author of text-books on logic and the history of philosophy. Rubinshtein, Leontyev and Lurye lectured on psychology. Courses in philosophy were given by Oizerman, Narski and others. We were deeply involved in the process of acquiring knowledge and we were carried away by it.

You were acquiring knowledge at first hand.

Yes, our teachers at the university were people whose names were the pride of Russian scholarship. And in our age group there were many brilliant and highly gifted young people. At times two-thirds of the student body consisted of boys and girls who had finished school with a gold or silver medal. In that post-war period the country was eager to get on with life and it was amazing then how much talent emerged from its depths, apparently drained dry by the war. I believe that it was not just by chance that there are quite a few academicians, doctors of science, professors and well-known statesmen, politicians, journalists, writers, economists and philologists today who were among those who graduated from the university in those days.

A student scientific society was active in the faculties and contributed its intellectual mite to the university's intellectual atmosphere. We all belonged to scientific societies.

Our programmes provided for the study of a very wide range of disciplines and subjects as well as specialized and classical literature. We spent hours in the library and reading-room. As soon as we woke in the Stromynka in the morning we had first of all to occupy a place in the reading-room and then go about our daily chores. We would 'stake out' a place, do our chores, and then return to the library to work. For the whole day. It was impossible to study or work in our living quarters: there were so many of us. We did our serious study in the reading-rooms and our university library and later, as senior students, in the Lenin Library. But we spent a great deal of time in the library at Stromynka.

The 'search for truth' continued at seminars, lectures and even at meetings. I remember with what exultation, at a meeting of the faculty's Komsomol organization, we 'discovered' the law of the negation of the negation – Hegel's law of dialectics, 'not recognized' in Stalin's works. The student meetings of that period! – they were already forerunners of the 'thaw'. The shell of inertia, silence and total fear was beginning to show cracks – at any rate at student gatherings. René Descartes's aphorism – 'I think: therefore I am' – was our slogan.

We did not discuss in those days the question of student self-government. But questions of the distribution of places in the hostel, the maintenance of order and the organization of our leisure time were decided with the very active participation of the students themselves. I remember how vigorously we defended the rights of the student family. At a conference of the university Young Communist organization a satirical newspaper appeared with a drawing of the rector trampling with a big boot on a marriage registration certificate – no more and no less! There was no room for the young married people to squeeze themselves in, and some student or graduate families already had children. They needed their own corner. It was an age-old problem. And it still exists. But at that time it was particularly acute.

Later, years later, when I was busy with scientific and teaching work, delivering lectures on philosophy, the history of atheism and religion, and ethics, I realized that the system and methods applied in education both in the schools and in higher institutions were bound by too many dogmas and constraints. It was that in particular that deprived me at the university of a lot of knowledge relating to the history of Russian and world culture. We were obliged to learn off by heart, for example, Stalin's speech at the 19th Congress of the Party, but we spent very little time studying the history of Russian humanitarian thought. Solovyov, Karamzin, Berdyayev and Florensky – it is only now that we have obtained real access to these philosophers, historians and writers. There was too much that was schematic and lifeless. And that, of course, deprived us of a great deal of knowledge. And again – it deprived us of the possibility of acquiring a real knowledge of a foreign language. At the university we learnt German and Latin. But later we did not have any opportunity to practice

foreign languages. I think that was a great loss for the whole
of my generation.

*I remember that there were quite a lot of surprised reactions when
it was discovered that it was possible to communicate in English with
the wife of M. S. Gorbachev, member of the Politburo and Secretary
of the Central Committee of the CPSU, when she accompanied her
husband on what was practically his first – in his new role – trip
abroad. It was unusual. High-ranking Soviet wives were usually
incapable of speaking English or German or anything else, and were
even more tongue-tied than their husbands.*

*I was also present and saw Raisa Gorbachev start up a conversation
in English with somebody abroad. True, it happened most frequently,
not with official persons or their 'other halves', but, as they say, with
'the man in the street'. With children, housewives or simply pedestrians
who recognized her and surrounded her in a tight ring everywhere,
on the streets and the squares and in the museums. There, in those
surroundings, she is not ashamed to use her English. In the same
way, incidentally, as the people around her, the public, are not
ashamed of their Russian: 'Raisa, Raisa!' can be heard on all sides.
If people are carrying placards or posters she also reads them out in a
loud voice. The people like it and so, I think, does she.*

I have never in my life felt envious because someone was
wearing a dress or other adornment that was more beautiful
than what I was wearing. But I really do envy people who
speak foreign languages fluently. And I still do. I learnt English late in life . . . I have tried to make up for lost time.

*We were discussing the atmosphere at Moscow University in those
days.*

Yes, despite all the obstacles there was also both radicalism
and creative teaching in the MGU, and they created an unrepeatable university atmosphere. You know, I would even be
more precise. With all the shortcomings in our system of
education, nevertheless the teaching and the social activities

in the MGU, unlike the other higher institutes, contained more radicalism, more excitement and more creativity, and so compensated in some way for the failings of the teaching process.

Thanks to the university and the atmosphere in it I acquired and have retained for ever a love of the student lecture hall and the company of young people. That's where I feel rather special. And, I have to confess, I always miss it. The very atmosphere of a young people's lecture hall, if you like, its very air, is liable at any moment to change into laughter, its special characteristic perhaps . . .

Whenever I go down into the Metro I immediately get submerged in the smell of my own youth. People who know say that it smells of warm rubber and dust, but it seems to me to smell of the 1960s. The smell of the Metro is linked with the smell of my own student youth – never in my life did I travel so frequently on the Metro as I did in those days.

It is possible that I have this attitude [to university life] also because I myself taught for many years. I don't know. But I believe it derives from that period, from my student years. Youth is an everlasting source of life, its worries, its fullness and its variety. The atmosphere prevailing in an audience of young people was similar wherever I worked, wherever I studied and wherever I visited, including places on the Soviet President's official trips. With young people all around you you feel younger yourself. I experienced that feeling in lecture halls in Stavropol, in Moscow University, the Charles University in Prague, in the Humboldt University in Berlin and at Stanford.

I carried that feeling away with me from Wellesley College in Boston. During the President's visit to the United States in June 1990 Mrs Barbara Bush and I travelled to Boston to the prestigious women's college, Wellesley. We attended the ceremonial presentation of degrees to graduates. I remember

a young girl, Christine Bicknell, speaking on behalf of the
graduates. I will read you an extract from her excellent speech
printed in a magazine that also published the speeches that
Barbara Bush and I made.

'Let us hope', said Christine, 'that in our years after
Wellesley we can have the courage to look as who we are and
to deal with the difficult issues that confront our lives. I believe
that we are strong women, well educated women, women who
have a commitment to bettering the world in which we live,
and I believe we will meet the challenges that the world holds
for us.'

You see how our approaches coincide! It is obviously the
spirit common to youth.

*It seemed to me that you and Mrs Barbara Bush faced the girl
students with a difficult choice.*

In what way?

*You personified for them two different paths. One is the path of
almost exclusive, self-sacrificing service to the family. The other is the
path of professional self-assertion combined with the management of a
family. In my view the young, intensely ambitious graduates were
impressed by the reference the head of the college made to your doctoral
thesis.*

But I recall something else — the wave of applause evoked
by Barbara's remark that she was sure that in that very auditorium was sitting somewhere, perhaps in the back row, the
future spouse of a future President of the United States — or
the future President herself.

*Indeed, you complemented each other very well not only on the
platform but also away from it.*

I have the warmest feelings and great respect for Mrs Barbara
Bush. I am impressed by her natural and direct manner with
people.

Young people approach life with the age-long confidence of being able to introduce something of their own, to achieve something and change things. That is why I love that eternally young student body, inspired with a bold sense of self-reliance.

It was at the university that I met Mikhail Sergeyevich. That is where our family originated.

I am often asked how we came to meet and how Mikhail Sergeyevich courted me. I suppose that is an important point in the reminiscences of every family. But for me there is something that is far more important and precious. Our relationship and our feelings were from the very beginning perceived by us . . . You know [*and she put her piece of paper down*] I have been thinking for a long time how to express it more precisely. And so — for me at any rate what is more precious is the following. Our relationship and our feeling were from the very outset perceived by us as a natural, inseparable part of our fate. We realized that our life would be unthinkable without each other. Our feelings were our very life itself.

Do you remember the poetess Natalia Krandieskaya? Wife of Aleksei Nikolayevich Tolstoy? She wrote these lines:

> They call the sky blue,
> They call the sun golden,
> They say that time is irreversible,
> They say the sea is boundless,
> They say a woman is beloved,
> They say death is inevitable,
> They say that truths are sacred,
> They say passions are fatal.
> What then shall I call my love,
> So as not to repeat the others?

Our first meeting was at a dance in the students' club in the

Stromynka. Mikhail Sergeyevich came along with his friends
Volodya Liberman and Yuri Topilin.

In those days, Georgi Vladimirovich, we did not study our
horoscopes. To tell the truth we didn't know horoscopes
existed. They are now all the rage. But we really didn't know
the meaning of Capricorn, one of the signs of the Zodiac,
under which I was born, or of Pisces, under which Mikhail
Sergeyevich was born. We didn't know if our relationship
would be lasting according to the signs or not. Whether our
marriage would be harmonious. We didn't even think about
it. It didn't worry us. Financial considerations didn't concern
us: legacies, family connections, somebody's position, protectionism. No. There were no legacies and no family connections. All we had was ourselves. All we had was with us.
Omnia mea mecum porto — 'Everything I have I carry with me'.

But I thought that was an English saying.

No, it's Latin. Like that other maxim: *Dum spiro, spero* — 'So
long as I breathe I hope'.

*In her speech, always correct, an occasional Latin word slips in,
revealing maybe what once attracted her to study at the university.*

We were friends for a long time before we got married.

I shall never forget the long walks we took around Moscow
— from the University and the Mokhovaya to Sokolniki and
the Stromynka. Just imagine what walking that involved!
Strolls along Gorky Street, the Petrovka and the Neglinnaya.
I mention the routes we were fond of. From the Lenin Library
to the Arbat, Kropotkinskaya and the Volkhonka. From the
Preobrazhensky Square (which was also on our favourite route
to Sokolniki) to the old building of the Mossoviet theatre. All
that was our romantic lesson in Muscovite geography.

Not to be forgotten are our joint excursions to visit exhibitions, the cinema and the theatre. Then there were concerts by Lemeshev, Kozlovsky, Aleksandrovich, Zvezdina,

Ognivtsev. Plays with the actors Mordvinov and Maretskaya. Performances by Nabatov.

Also not to be forgotten was our beloved Sokolniki park with its deer pond (I don't know if it is there now, but it was then), and its winter skating-rink. Have you ever been on a Moscow rink? Which one?

Ten years ago I took the children to Sokolniki.

You know, in our day they played just one and the same record at the skating-rink. I am trying to remember what it was. For some reason I haven't come across it anywhere. 'White snowflakes are falling: Catch me up, catch me up.' Yes, they played it only at the rink.

I too remember the repeated 'Catch me up'.

I have never heard that tune again. I can't recall it. But it was certainly at the Sokolniki ice-rink that it was played.

I cannot forget either how we welcomed the New Year – 1954 – in the Hall of Columns. The fir-tree and the music. Young faces all around, and we were there. I remember that people seemed to notice us.

You were a good-looking couple, no doubt.

They were sort of drawn towards us. And it gave rise to a reciprocal feeling of warmth and friendliness. Perhaps it was a general holiday – of youth, of the happiness of youth? The New Year celebration in the Hall of Columns in 1954. But perhaps it was also connected with the fact that it was the year 1954 – that the old life had been left somewhere behind us in 1953.

We got married in the autumn of 1953. Our marriage took place in the Sokolniki registry office, on the other bank of the Yauza. But when we returned to Moscow later and went to look for it we could no longer find the office. They had transferred it to the Wedding Palace. There is now some kind of municipal services agency. But in the past the registry office was immediately opposite our hostel.

All very logical – the student hostel and the marrriage office opposite.

The building has been preserved. It's a large building. On the other bank, in the Preobrazhenka, there are very large buildings. The registry office was on the ground floor.

We celebrated our wedding in the Stromynka. It was a student affair, very jolly, with singing, drinking and dancing. Mikhail Sergeyevich earned the money needed for the wedding, for a new suit for himself and a 'wedding-dress' for me (not a proper wedding-dress – we'll put the word in inverted commas – they didn't make special dresses to measure in those days. And there was no wedding-ring. But the dress was new). To tell the truth, our parents knew nothing of our intentions. We let them know at the last moment. That shows how little young people care for their parents' opinion – both then and now. So there you are – we're having a wedding, we don't need any money, we've got some. And that's the only announcement. Well, our parents didn't have much money either. But we lived with a constant feeling of responsibility to them. For example, I tried all my life not to overburden my mother and father in any way, not to ask for more than they could manage, and not to take much from them. After all, I was the eldest, and they had two other children and they didn't find life easy.

Mikhail Sergeyevich earned money in the summer as a combine driver harvesting the wheat. True, we didn't have enough money to buy me a pair of shoes. I had to borrow shoes from a girl friend in our group. But there was the dress – it was our first joint acquisition. The dress was made in a real Moscow tailor's shop that I remember very well, near the Kirovskaya Metro station.

In the summer of 1953, before our wedding, Mikhail

Sergeyevich and I parted for three months. His practical work in his training as a lawyer coincided with the holiday period. He did it in his own Red Guard district. In those days it was called the Molotov district. We spent those months waiting for letters from each other.

I had long since noticed that Raisa Maksimovna had those letters. As soon as we had set up the tape recorder and taken up our positions for our conversation — she at the table and I in a chair opposite. I had long been eyeing those sheets of paper taken out of a lined exercise book, known for some reason as 'general'. I had realized long ago that they were letters. Whatever they are written on, letters always give off something that makes it possible for you immediately to determine: that is a letter. If everything that has spent some time in a person's hands bears in some way the imprint of humanity, then a letter is doubly so. Especially an old one, so thin you can see through it. I myself still have some of those faded letters. But I do not have and there never were any letters from my mother: she was still illiterate when she died.

I had of course already guessed whom the letters lying on the table were from. I had already been eyeing them on the sly but they had never come into my hands. My interlocutor had, of course, noticed my curiosity but she had not suggested that I might look at them or hold them even if not to read them. On the contrary, throughout our conversation her hand had, consciously or unconsciously, rested on the little bundle of letters with their edges stained by time.

What does Vysotsky say? I don't like other people to read my letters, peering over my shoulder?

In that case that man of character was singing the views of this woman of character.

As I re-read these letters from Mikhail Sergeyevich today, these lines written on faded scraps of paper — how many years have passed! — written sometimes in ink, sometimes in pencil, sometimes in the steppe on a combine harvester, sometimes in the district prosecutor's office in the lunch break or late at

night after work, I think again and again, not only about the
feeling that brought us together in our youth. I also think
that the choice we made about life and our path through it
that began in those early years was not a matter of chance.

I would like to quote some passages from two or three of
Mikhail Sergeyevich's letters. Not the whole letters, because
they contain pages intended only for me – and they will depart
when I do. Yes, there are things that are intended for me
alone, however many years pass. But I will read you something from them. Look – this one still has the mark on it –
'Prosecutor's Office, Molotov Region'.

And I thought it was you who had placed those marks on them.

Nothing of the sort. Nobody has touched these letters. I've
just decided to re-read them. Look – 'Prosecutor's Office of
the Molotov District'. Even the date – 20st of June, 1953.
He was working at the Prosecutor's Office and began to write
a letter on the first piece of paper that came to hand.

'. . . I am so depressed by the situation here. And I feel it
especially keenly every time I receive a letter from you. It
brings with it so much that is good, dear, close and understandable. And one feels all the more keenly how disgusting
my surroundings are here. Especially the manner of life of the
local bosses. The acceptance of convention, subordination,
with everything predetermined, the open impudence of
officials and the arrogance. When you look at one of the local
bosses you see nothing outstanding apart from his belly. But
what aplomb, what self-assurance and the condescending,
patronizing tone! The contempt for science. Consequently a
disparaging attitude to young specialists. I read recently in a
newspaper a note from a livestock expert, a man called Movsis-
yan, a graduate from the Stavropol agricultural institute. It is
really shameful. You can see your own fate in what happened
to him. The man arrived here with great plans and set about
his work with great enthusiasm, but he very soon began to

feel that everyone was absolutely indifferent to it all. They all laughed at him and mocked him.

'Such passivity and conservatism . . .'

She interrupts her reading and says:

Thirty-seven years have passed. Did I ever think then that I would read it out? Aloud . . .

She speaks in such a tone that I begin to fear that the reading will be brought to an end. But a minute later she resumes, quoting from another letter:

'I have been chatting with a lot of young specialists. They are all very dissatisfied. As usual I have a great deal, a very great deal of work. I am normally at my desk till late. At night I write my "diary", consisting of short comments. Later they will be signed by the procurator. I have been nowhere else in this place. But, to tell the truth, there's nowhere to go: it's all so boring. If it weren't for the work . . .'

As you are reading I seem to see a young man who has been sent out of Moscow after the university with what you call his fierce radicalism, his 'ideas' and his enthusiasm straight into the depths of the provinces, the 'land of Nod'.

The Land of Nod? I'm not sure about that . . . But where were we? Yes — 'Please write to me. I always long for them to come, your letters. It is as if you yourself were coming to me. And I really need you here. Yours ever, Mikhail.'

And this [*she picks up some other sheets of paper from the table*] is a letter from the fields. He was working on a combine harvester and apparently wrote it with interruptions on two or three occasions: 'Rayechka! We have just begun to gather in the harvest at full steam. It's very difficult in these conditions . . .'

That was probably why he wrote in pencil, because he was working in the fields?

Probably. [*She reads another letter*]. 'The wheat crop is plenti-
ful and good, but with a lot of weeds in it. This has really
complicated work on the combine. The day's work on the
combine works out like this: We rise long before sunrise. We
prepare the combine for work and give it a technical service.
That takes about three or four hours, and then we start harvesting the grain . . . We carry on as long as it is possible, that
is as long as the wheat is dry. For harvesting at night there is
a special light . . . Every day we spend twenty hours on our
feet. And we work in a horrible dust and on scorching hot
metal. The sun beats down unbearably. We've had so many
very hot days – thirty-five or thirty-six degrees. It makes you
want to rip everything off. There's nothing to breathe. I will
end here . . . How I shall send this letter I don't know. I
wrote on the seventeenth. When I shall send it I don't know
for sure . . .' Well, there's no need to read on.

And have your letters to him been preserved?

Do you really think men preserve letters as we women do?
I have kept them all, every single one . . . I will read you a
passage from one more letter. The same exercise book, the
same pencil. Apparently he wrote a couple of days later: 'You
were asking about the building of the house . . . I can't honestly call it a house . . . It's just an ordinary peasant cottage.
It has now been roofed with tiles and the windows have been
put in. In general it is suitable for living in. The trouble is
that I still can't get hold of timber for the floors . . .'

Very topical!

Yes, unfortunately. Throughout our life we suffer from
shortages. By the way, it was a friend of my father's working
in the village Soviet who helped him to buy my first coat. But
we have digressed.
[*She continues reading from Gorbachev's letter.*]
'We have even been in Stalingrad, but to no purpose. The

rendering of the walls has been finished and they will be whitewashed later. Meanwhile we are all still in the apartment and it's very inconvenient in several ways. Mama is particularly tired of it.

'I know, Rayechka, I haven't written to you. Our work-team consists almost entirely of Gorbachevs. Papa is the combine operator, I do the steering and Semen Grigorievich Gorbachev is the tractor driver. There is a girl on the straw collector – Anna Mikhailovna Gorbachev, and the grain is transported from the combine in a truck by Vasili Alekseyevich Gorbachev. Our team is known as "The Gorbachevs". Papa, Semen and Vasili are cousins . . . I must finish now . . . Warmest greetings from the sphere of production to the sphere of the intellect.'

Did he send that to you at home? Were you on holiday?

No, I was at the University. He had gone off to do his practical training, and I had still some examination to pass.

In that same year, 1953, we moved into a student hostel on the Lenin Hills. It was a new part of the University, built in the 1950s and later which included lecture halls, administrative buildings and common rooms, libraries, clubs, canteens, a polyclinic and an up-to-date and, as it seemed to us, amazingly comfortable hostel for students and graduates. It was all very well done. Everyone had a separate, though tiny, furnished room. Two people shared a shower and a lavatory.

Our transfer to the new university building coincided with our completing our studies at the MGU. This was a very different stage in our life as students. Mikhail Sergeyevich and I were now always together. We wrote our theses and prepared for taking the state examinations. We read a great deal. We studied the German language. We even translated together some of the texts we used. I had the opportunity of observing at close quarters with what enthusiasm Gorbachev, student at the law faculty of the MGU, set about his studies, always trying to get to the essence, to the very heart of the matter.

We gave serious thought to our future. In my last years as a student I was often ill: a cold that I did nothing about complicated by rheumatism. The doctors insisted on a change of climate. After graduation I was recommended for post-graduate study. I passed the examination and began my studies. Mikhail Sergeyevich was offered a choice: to take a job in Moscow or to do post-graduate work. But we decided to drop everything and go to work in Stavropol, his birth-place.

Raisa Maksimovna fell silent, lost in thought.

Of course, there is a sort of secret. The secret of the feelings and the laws that unite two people. Especially people who become indispensable to each other. And it is beyond the powers of people or of science to penetrate that secret. And it is a good thing that there is something secret in the world.

As I return to those years in my thoughts I ask myself again: what was Mikhail Sergeyevich like then, in his youth, when he came into my life? What kind of person was he? An intelli-gent, reliable friend? Yes. A man who had his own opinion and was capable of defending it vigorously? Yes. In my youth I came up against the fact – and it was one of my very painful disappointments – that some people are not able to stand up for their own opinions, and do not even have such opinions. But he was a man who had an opinion of his own and was capable of defending it and standing up for it with dignity. But that's not all.

Today, Georgi Vladimirovich, I am thinking about some-thing different. In the fierce struggle now going on between good and evil, loyalty and treachery, hope and disillusion,

generosity and venality, vengefulness, I think of his inborn
love of his fellow-men. His respect for people. And it really
is inborn. It is not, after all, something that can be cultivated
in a person, I am quite convinced of that. And it is not to be
acquired along with a degree, any kind of degree. Respect for
people and for their dignity as human beings . . . I think
about his inability (my God, how many times have I thought
about it!) to assert himself at the expense of others, their
dignity and rights. No, he is not capable of asserting himself
by destroying another person. The person next to him.

I can see his face and his eyes. We have been together
for thirty-seven years. Everything in this life changes. But a
constant hope lives in my heart: that he, my husband, should
remain just as he was when he came into my life in our youth.
Manly and steadfast, strong and kind. And that he should be
able in the end to sing his favourite songs again – and, let me
tell you again, he can sing and loves it. And that he should
be able to read his favourite poems and to laugh, openly and
sincerely, as he always did.

*The conversation was over. I quietly put the tapes away in envelopes
and numbered them. Raisa Maksimovna remained for a time sitting
there in silence, having pushed to one side the many pieces of paper,
all covered with notes and scribbles. She stared thoughtfully ahead
and raised her hand to her temple. Her face had become quite pale.
Her last words were surprisingly like a prayer . . .*

*In the intervals at that memorable Congress of People's Deputies in
December I had observed how the Deputies had appealed to her on
more than one occasion:*

*'Raisa Maksimovna – why do you stay here listening to the
debates? Just to make yourself suffer? You might as well be at home
watching it on the television.'*

*She did not go away, of course. It has been said more than once
that she is practically always present when her husband speaks in
public, both in the Soviet Union and abroad. At foreign press confer-*

ences she sits somewhere in the front row. In this country she doesn't sit in the front row in sight of the television cameras, but wherever he speaks he has no keener listener. But she listens not only to him but also to the crowded hall behind her. It's not an easy fate, especially in Russia — to have all eyes focussed on you and people talking and expressing opinions about you.

I believe he senses her presence in the hall even in the heat of an argument, and I don't think the Soviet political scene has known such a spirited orator since Lenin's days — when it seems as though he sees nobody apart from his immediate opponent.

'A secret not subject to the judgement of others . . .' As with any couple. But fate has decreed that these two have a much larger audience. And that means the judgement is more severe.

When American journalists once asked Gorbachev which serious questions he discussed with his wife, he thought for a moment and replied: 'All of them.'

Not everyone in his place would have permitted himself such manly directness, although, frankly speaking, are there any serious questions that we do not discuss with our wives? Of course not. Only some of us admit it while others prefer not to, reckoning that in that way they increase their masculinity and independence in the eyes of others.

Gorbachev behaves very chivalrously in his relations with his wife, I certainly would not be so stupid as to suggest that this is a result of perestroika. I am not looking for any link here. I simply see a symbol. A sign. Although in Russia one's attitude to women, and especially to one's own wife, may also be an aspect of perestroika and even demand a certain degree of courage from a man. At least in the Russia that I know best, because I was born and grew up in it, the old attitude towards women in my Russia is still very much alive.

Raisa Maksimovna allows herself to express her own individuality in the form primarily of a sense of her own worth. Mikhail Sergeyevich treats this with invariable quiet respect. It seems as though much respect forms part of some code of honour that he observes with enviable self-control, even in situations where another person would have long ago burst into hysterics. If I were more daring I would say that there *is in the relations between these two people, who have both sprung from 'the people', a sort of aristocratism which I have come across frequently in good, traditional peasant families.*

In one of the letters addressed to Raisa Gorbachev I read: 'Thank you! Thanks to you and your husband the image of Soviet woman is changing in Russia and the world. She is regaining her dignity . . .'

Gorbachev is paying his people the long-standing debts incurred by others and this may be his most dramatic problem. He is also paying a debt called 'human dignity'.

As I left I said some nice things about her daughter, whom I had just met. Perhaps it was because I myself tend to judge people as good or bad by one single indicator — by their attitude toward my children.

Thank you. Would you like me to tell you an amusing story? When our first granddaughter was born my husband and I went to see Irina in the maternity home. As we entered the vestibule I said to the nurse: 'Open the door wider — grandma has arrived!' The nurse opened the door, looked to see who was behind me and said: 'But where is the grandmother?' [*And her brown eyes flashed with amusement*].

You see? And you said it was diet.

That was a long time ago. [*Smiling, she rose from the table.*]

As for the last Congress that we were talking about, it ended up to the advantage of the President. After the first day the course of the gathering took a sharp turn and Raisa Gorbachev remained to witness, not only some of the President's most difficult and dramatic minutes, but also the way the crisis was overcome. The chain of cause and effect here is unbelievably complicated, but it really seems to me that simple human courage, loyalty and patience also deserve to be rewarded.

'A prophet is not without honour save in his own country'. To bring the subject of this chapter to an end I will quote one other letter:

Allow me, Mr General Secretary, to thank you for the
hospitality you have shown us and to wish good health
to yourself and Mrs Gorbachev, whose presence at your
side created a new perception of your country – of charm
and culture. It was especially agreeable for me and my
wife to see her here . . .

François Mitterrand.

CHAPTER FOUR

The Test of Real Life

Raisa Maksimovna, our last conversation ended at the point at which you decided not to do post-graduate work and chose to move to Stavropol.

Yes, I gave up the idea of doing post-graduate work, although I had already passed the examination for it and had joined the course. Mikhail Sergeyevich also turned down Moscow. We chose Stavropol, his birthplace.

Stavropol — they say that every human being cherishes in his heart his own little homeland, the place where he was born and grew up. If that's so, can you imagine what sort of 'little' homeland I have? The whole Soviet Union — so many moves from one place to another that I went through in childhood. But Mikhail Sergeyevich's little homeland is, of course, the Stavropol region.

What did I want to tell you about Stavropol? It's an amazing region! A region of an abundance of sunshine, wheat and gardens. And of the sunflower that moves around to face the hot sun throughout the day. A region of wonderful mountains and steppes. The steppes full of smells. What do the steppes of the Stavropol region smell of? You, Georgi Vladimirovich, ought to remember.

In my birthplace in the summer the steppes smell of the grasses.

That's right, and of thyme as well. Apart from that it's a region of health-giving, healing waters, sources of mineral waters, a very rare mixture produced by the sands of the desert and the mountain glaciers. If you have ever been in Kislovodsk you have probably seen Lermontov's words carved in the rock: 'I love the Caucasus like the sweet melody of my homeland.'

It was in Stavropol, the centre of the region, that Mikhail Sergeyevich and I arrived after completing university, as young specialists, full of plans and hopes. It marked the beginning of our working lives, the start of a totally new life in a new environment.

You asked me, Georgi Vladimirovich, what I thought of Stavropol after Moscow. Both Moscow and Stavropol are cities. But what a difference between them! They say that the first impression you have of a person is the most lasting. I don't know about persons, but it is certainly very true when it comes to cities. My first impression of Stavropol remains in my memory for ever.

Stavropol struck me by its greenery. It is a flood of green. It seemed as though the city had been decked out in luxurious green clothes. Lombardy poplars and such a lot of chestnuts. And willows and oaks and elms. And lilac. And flowers every-where. In the autumn this apparel gives the city a beautiful crimson-gold, touchingly gentle look. The appearance of the city at that time is the very image of autumn. I have never come across anywhere a better autumn and I believe that autumn is by far the best season of the year in the Stavropol region. In my childhood I loved the springtime – springtime in the Urals with its babbling brooks and floodwater. But in the Stavropol region I came to like the autumn. Spring is quickly over here, whereas the autumn is long, very colourful and warm.

I was impressed by the city itself, the centre of the region, which had a certain restraint and tranquillity about it. The main square, the streets and the houses seemed to have pre-served the spirit of our ancestors – Russians and Cossacks who came here two hundred years ago.

Oh yes, when I spoke about the greenery I forgot one detail. Struck as I was in my first days there by its beauty and plenty, it was only later that I learned that the beauty is the city's 'hobby' and a good and long-standing tradition among the people of Stavropol. Later I enjoyed playing my part in keeping the city green.

In the Stavropol region every little town is 'cultivated' like a garden.

I remember there was even a film made about Stavropol – *The Greenest Town in Russia.* The second thing that struck me was the measured pace of life and the patriarchal quiet in what was the centre of one of the country's biggest regions. The pace of life was dictated by the fact that people walked everywhere. There was no transport problem, no 'rush hour' in those days in Stavropol. Wherever you were going – to work, to the shops, to the baths, the hairdresser, the polyclinic or the market – it was possible to get there on foot. Only the central square and a few streets were paved. Only a few administrative buildings and blocks of flats had central heating. Drinking water had to be carried from standpipes. And in the very centre of the town, opposite the teachers' college, there was an enormous sea of mud. All the year round it stayed there and there was no way, on foot or on wheels, that you could get through it. It was like Gogoli's 'Mirgorod'. Of course, Stavropol is a very different place today.

More than three decades have passed. Modern industry has arrived, new scientific, educational and cultural centres have been built, and the population has almost doubled. That fact alone, of course, has changed the content and the rhythm of life in the city and its appearance. But at that time, for the centre of a vast region in Russia, which in those years included two autonomous regions, Stavropol was excessively provincial.

The cinema was called, of course, the Giant, as in every small town. There was the Lermontov theatre of drama, whose repertoire we knew backwards in the course of two or three months. In that theatre I knew by heart everything they performed. There was the regional library, an orchestra, a museum of local history and two more cinemas – the October and the Motherland – and a few clubs and film-showing rooms. That was all the cultural facilities there were.

You arrived in Stavropol with a university education obtained in the capital, in Moscow. In those days that was very rare. How did your workmates regard you? What were relations like where you were employed?

There weren't any.

I don't understand, Raisa Maksimovna.

There's nothing to understand – I had big problems trying to find a job. In the first few months in Stavropol I simply couldn't find any work. Then for a year and a half I had a job I was not trained for. Then I had two years of work in my speciality but with no real rights. Either I was paid by the hour or on half-salary, with occasional dismissal when the staff was reduced. So there's your 'person with a university education from Moscow' and 'a rarity in those days'. Yes – actually I did not have a permanent job for four years.

Why?

I think there were two reasons. I believe that in those years there were problems throughout the country with the employment of specialists with a higher education in the humanities. I knew, for example, that in Stavropol at that time about seventy per cent of the teachers were working part time. But no less important in my view was the second reason.

Yes, it's true – in Stavropol in those days there were practically no specialists with a university education, certainly not ones from Moscow university. I don't know exactly, so I stress the word 'practically'. Well, perhaps there were two or three.

In the faculties of the colleges where my professional training might have been used the appropriate disciplines were taught by people with teaching qualifications obtained very often by correspondence. As a rule they were graduates of their own Stavropol teachers' college. I do not wish to throw any doubt on their professional qualifications. When I came later to work among them I met people who were carrying out important scientific research, and were doing it very capably, delivered excellent lectures, enjoyed the well-deserved affection of the students, and gave themselves over entirely to their profession. But there were a good many who were simply not able, and who didn't want, to engage in research of any kind. They didn't want to and weren't capable. Such people delivered lectures prepared by someone else at some other time, used other people's material, and had noticeable difficulty in pronouncing philosophical categories and concepts. Great difficulty. But the institute regarded them as 'its own' people – people they knew, who knew its ways and were easy to manage. It made them better off financially. For in our country the rate of pay remains stable, depending on the position and the title, but not on the quantity and certainly not the quality of the work performed.

I even came across people who were quite incapable of delivering lectures but who nevertheless received a lecturer's pay. They received the pay, but other people delivered their lectures. Competitions held to fill vacant places on the staff were conducted as a pure formality. The college did its best to hold on to its own people. Moreover, specialists invited to Stavropol from outside would need accommodation. Where would one find it? Every collective had more than enough people waiting for flats. Even if the students were not satisfied with the quality of the lectures and the seminars, there was nothing considered terrible in that. They were obliged to attend the course just the same, irrespective of whether the course suited them or not.

The quality of the teaching, the system employed and the way the teaching was organized affected the training of specialists throughout the country and not only in Stavropol. Everything in the colleges was strictly controlled. Everything that was and was not permitted – the relationship between the students and the teachers, the list of members of the staff, the teaching load, and the hours devoted to the various disciplines. The number of scientists and teachers employed by the college was always determined by the size of the student intake. It was more to their advantage to take in more school-leavers and to release exactly as many as were admitted. Otherwise the staff had to be cut down. This alone can explain certain episodes in my teaching practice, about one of which I want to tell you now.

A correspondence student was having his third attempt to pass the examination. I had a talk with him, trying to extract an answer at least to the very simplest and elementary questions. I tried to get him to say what philosophy was. Alas, all my efforts were in vain. Then, suddenly, when I was already exhausted, he said with feeling: 'Raisa Maksimovna, I am so sorry for you.' 'You are sorry for me,' I asked in astonishment. 'Well, why do you get so upset? You are wasting time. This is the third time you try. But I do the same with everyone. I do all my subjects like that. True, they all give me a "three", and I am through. And everyone's happy. What's the difference?' he asked me.

And how did you mark him?

I gave him a 'three' as well. I acted against my conscience – not for the first or only time.

I am glad that we are giving serious thought today to the problems that have piled up in Russia in the field of education of every kind – general, vocational and higher education. We are seeking ways to make it more democratic, to improve all its branches, to raise the quality of the teaching, and to raise the status of higher education in our country. So much has become a pure formality. We have been training specialists without knowing what they are for. The number of degrees we have created! Many a time I have asked in the college: why do we award a degree to a person who is not really educated either in the professional sense or in the general sense? When he turns up to work with his degree he will demand the same rights as a properly educated person, a real specialist in great demand. You see, it's a vicious circle – the production of the unwanted.

There is a great need for major changes in this field, and it is a good thing that they have already begun. Take, for example, the President's latest decisions about granting autonomy to institutions of higher education. These are tentative moves towards improving a hitherto stagnant system. Even in the past, experience was, of course, being gained, traditions established and progress made, but there was also a good deal of stagnation.

Raisa Maksimovna, let us return to Stavropol.

Sorry, I didn't keep to the subject, I digressed. The subject of higher education is a professional weakness with me . . . Stavropol. Mikhail Sergeyevich arrived there from Moscow in the same year as he finished at the university and a little sooner than I did. He arrived with a lawyer's degree at the disposition of the regional prosecutor's office. But he worked there no more than ten days. He wrote to me: 'No, working in the prosecutor's office is not for me . . . I met some comrades with whom I used to work in the Komsomol.' And in another letter: 'In view of my experience of work in the Komsomol, both in school and university, they have offered me a job in the regional Komsomol organization. You know what my attitude is to work in the Komsomol.' And again: 'I had a long and unpleasant conversation with the regional pros-ecutor.' And in another letter: 'After more talks with me and after berating me in every way, they have agreed to my leaving to join the regional Komsomol.' The next sentence was: 'I have been confirmed in the job of deputy head of the department of agitation and propaganda.'

Incidentally, the regional prosecutor at the time was B. N. Petukhov, the man with whom Mikhail Sergeyevich had the 'long and unpleasant conversation'. Petukhov is an outstanding man. He has devoted almost fifty years to work as a prosecutor and investigator, and he has written a number of interesting accounts of his work. He presented inscribed copies of two of his books, published in 1970 and 1981, to Mikhail Sergeyevich. And he wrote a letter which I will also quote to you: 'I think today with tremendous satisfaction that I acted correctly when I did not stand in the way of your career.'

He was a far-sighted man!

Mikhail Sergeyevich's pay amounted to 1000 roubles a month in 'old' money, as we say.

That's supposed to be 100 roubles in 'new' money.

After paying various taxes and membership fees to all sorts of organizations we were left with 840 roubles. I remember it well, because, bearing in mind my lengthy 'unemployment', that money was for a long time our only income. Apart from some food parcels that Mikhail Sergeyevich's parents sent us occasionally from the country. They were not able to help us more than that.

When he worked in the Komsomol Mikhail Sergeyevich frequently had to make trips round the region. On one such 'business trip' he wrote to me . . .

He wrote to you from such trips?

Yes – is there anything surprising in that?

Nowadays, as far as I know, men don't write to their wives even

*from trips abroad. And he wasn't far away — only travelling round
the region.*

It depends on what kind of husband. So in one of his letters
he wrote the following: '. . . I don't know how many times
I've been to Privolnoye hearing them talk of just twenty
roubles — where were they going to find such a sum? Despite
the fact that my father works day and night the whole year
round. I am simply overwhelmed with shame. Honestly I can't
keep back my tears. At the same time you can't help thinking
that, after all, they still don't live too badly. But what about
the others? There's a great deal yet to be done. Our parents
and thousands like them really deserve a better life . . .'

Those words seemed to me like something out of Ovechkin's Provincial Routine.

He was a very keen student of the life around him: it was
as though he wanted to make up for the time spent studying
in Moscow. His worries didn't give him any peace and he had
a constant need to express himself, which was probably one of
the things that prompted him to write so many letters to me
when he was on his trips. They were really like studies in
'provincial routine'.

Life wasn't so very cheap in those days. Out of our 800
roubles we paid two hundred for the flat, a little room in a
private house that we rented.

Whereabouts was it?

I will show you a photo of the house now, and you can
guess where it is, since you also call yourself a Stavropolian.

*Raisa Gorbachev selected a little snapshot from a bundle of photos
she had prepared. The snapshot was quite faded. In the foreground
there were trees — wherever you take a picture in Stavropol there will
always be trees in the foreground — through which you could see a
typical Stavropol 'private' house built of the local limestone. I once*

rented space in such a building. Even in my day at the end of the 1960s three-quarters of Stavropol consisted of such houses, all over-grown with hops and grape vines. So just try and guess where that one is — on the Osetinka, the Tashla or near the Lower market?

I suppose I must be a bad Stavropolian, Raisa Maksimovna, or I left Stavropol too long ago — in 1973. I don't recognize the street. Tell me what it is.

Do I need to? The house is still there. But I wonder whether we ought to attract attention to it and disturb the peace of the people living there who are relations of our former land-lord. No, better that I should tell you in greater detail about the little room that we rented there and which I can still see so vividly.

Well, if that's how you feel . . .

We had difficulty in finding room in it for our 'possessions' at the time. A bed, a table, two chairs and two huge boxes full of books. In the centre of the room was a huge stove. We had to buy our own coal and wood. I used to cook on a paraffin stove in the narrow corridor.

But our 'apartment' had its advantages. The little room was very light, with three windows all looking out on to the garden. It was a big and very beautiful garden. And the owners were good and kind and I count that as another good thing about the room. They were former teachers now living on a pension. The old man was very strict and not very talkative, unlike his wife and daughter. And it was only when he had had a drop too much to drink and was not quite sober that he would instruct me that I must 'look soberly at life'.

It was in that room on the 6th of January 1957, on the eve of the Orthodox Christmas, that our daughter Irinka was born. At the maternity home they entered into her medical record: 'Weight at birth — 3 kilograms 300 grams. Height 50 centi-metres. Weight on leaving maternity home — 3 kilograms 100

'Invitation to an Interview' — for years I have been asked to write a book about myself, but it was only after travelling around the world, being showered with questions, especially from women, that I decided that it was something I must do

Wives of the leaders of the
Party and the state, 1986:
First row, left to right:
  Z. I. Ligacheva
  L. S. Ryzhkova
  R. M. Gorbacheva
  L. D. Gromyko
  Z. M. Chebrikova
second row:
  V. A. Zimyanina
  L. I. Zaikova
  N. N. Solomentseva
  A. G. Shcherbitskaya
  B. I. Ponomareva
  N. R. Shevardnadze
  Z. Sh. Kunayeva
  E. N. Nikonova
  M. S. Sokolova
  T. V. Kapitonova
  N. I. Yeltsina

Meeting in the fields
Kazakhstan, 1991

The World Congress of
Women, 1987

Residential home for war veterans and invalids, Moscow 1991

Opening of the American exhibition in Moscow, with Armand Hammer, the American millionaire and friend of Lenin

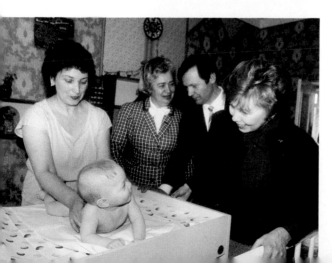

At a children's home in Donetsk in the Ukraine, 1989

Meeting the Polish people
in the streets of Warsaw, 1988

'My Hopes' –
Mikhail Sergeyevich's
vision of *perestroika* has
introduced new
thinking to improve
every aspect of life in
our country

With President Mitterrand
in Paris, 1985

The United States of
America, 1990

When presidents
smile. . .

With Deng Xiaoping, the
veteran Chinese Communist
leader, in 1989

A pre-school children's home,
Latvia 1987

Irina and Ksenia at a Parade in
the Red Square

In search of mushrooms, 1990

Meeting Japan

With Nancy Reagan
in the Kremlin
during former US
President Reagan's
visit for his summit
meeting

Japan – your health!

With Barbara Bush at
Wellesley College in the
United States in 1990 –
after the generous
reception I received here,
I finally decided that I
must write about myself

Federal German Republic, 1990

In the Svyato-Danilov monastery
in Moscow on the eve of
the Orthodox Easter, 1990

In the Sverdlovsk region

Mikhail Sergeyevich
in one of his now-
famous walkabouts,
with the people of
the Arctic town
of Norilsk, 1988

grams. A healthy child.' I remember that entry by heart: in those happy days the words were music to my ears.

In the same year, thanks to efforts by Mikhail Sergeyevich's colleagues, we obtained a 'government apartment' in a building in which the two top storeys were intended as housing. The ground floor was to serve as offices. But because of the difficult housing situation the lower floor gradually came to be used as housing too. Our 'two-roomed' apartment, which had previously served as an office and reception room, was the last bastion to fall. More precisely — for someone or some department it was a defeat, but for our family it was a victory. Consequently the whole floor became one huge unit of eight apartments with a common kitchen at the end of the corridor and a communal toilet.

That means you lived in a communal apartment?

Yes, our neighbours were a demobilized lieutenant-colonel, a mechanic from the garment factory, a welder, a hospital employee . . . They were all people with families. And there were four single women, two living together and two in separate rooms. And we — Mikhail Sergeyevich and I — for the first time in our lives had our own apartment.

It was a little sovereign state with a great variety of sovereign subjects to use modern terminology. It was a state with its own unwritten but universally understood laws. And in it people worked, loved, separated, drank like Russians, quarrelled like Russians and made it up again like Russians. In the evenings they played dominoes. We celebrated our birthdays together. To speak disparagingly of others or to display arrogance was completely out of the question. It was a sort of direct, natural, human world.

Mikhail Sergeyevich used to make fun of me. Interestingly enough, he was then already using the sort of parliamentary jargon that we use today. In one letter — he wrote so often because we had no telephone as in those days few people had telephones – he wrote: 'It is up to you to maintain diplomatic relations with the other sovereign units. I hope you will take pride in conducting our foreign policy. But don't forget the principle of mutual interest.'

Really a quite modern formulation!

In that house I got to know people with whom I maintained good relations throughout our years in Stavropol. One such person was Zoya Vasilievna Karetnikova, wife of the lieutenant-colonel who had not had an easy life but was generously gifted. They had moved to Stavropol from Lvov on account of the state of health of the husband, Pyotr Fyodorovich. He is no longer with us – may he rest in peace.

Because her husband was a military man Zoya Vasilievna had been unable to complete her studies as a geologist. She was from Moscow. She had golden fingers and a natural artistic taste. I have to tell you that there were no tailors or dress shops in Stavropol, and for twenty years Zoya Vasilievna made and remade everything I and my family wore. I was friendly with her for twenty years and her loyal and constant customer.

I believe you continued to have her make things for you even after you became the wife of the 'first man'.

Yes.

Stavropol is a relatively small town, and I have heard it said that the wife of the First Secretary was always well turned out.

That only goes to confirm that Zoya Vasilievna really did have golden fingers.

And that was your special dressmakers?

You could say that. In Stavropol I also got to know Ksenia Mikhailovna Yefremova, an employee in the garment factory. Her fiancé was killed in the Finnish war, and she was left completely alone. I do not know, of course, whether my former neighbours and kind helpers will ever come to read this little book. But I want to thank each one of them. And special thanks to Ksenia Mikhailovna for the help she gave me at a very difficult time in my life when I was doing a job, writing a thesis, going on long trips and when my daughter was often very sick.

We all come from the people. In the early 1970s I heard an unexpected continuation of the quotation: how are we to return to them? The relationship between those who 'emerged' and the environment, the 'people', from whom they emerged, can be extremely complicated. Too often the dominant factor becomes the almost complete mutual alienation. Some of the big bosses or wives of the big bosses don't want to be reminded where they have come from. Others detect that reluctance. For some reason it is not the bosses themselves but their wives who most frequently do not wish to be reminded.

In this case the situation is quite different. I long ago noticed Raisa Maksimovna's ability, without special effort and without trying to ingratiate herself, to understand and accept the world into which she was born. The natural relationship she had with that world and a certain feeling of obligation towards it has long been characteristic of the Russian intelligensia. I don't expect you to be affected by this; I just ask you to note in your memory for the future the 'communal flat dwellers' of 1957. How often, as we move 'forward and upwards', we cast off our old friends like old clothes.

For me work was not just a means of earning money. It was also a cause without which I would have thought my life was a failure. Student lectures, seminars, academic conferences, meetings and debates – can you imagine how much effort, time, intellectual tension and even sleepless nights they demanded? But they gave me a great deal. They gave me the incomparable feeling of moral satisfaction.

Then there were the arguments and discussions we had in our spare time – in the student hostel, on the collective farm, where we were all, teachers and students alike, sent to gather in the corn, the grapes and the potatoes. They went on too in

my flat, where my students also came. We discussed everything – new plays in the theatre, new films, events in the life
of the college, the region and the country. We argued till we
were hoarse, of course, about the meaning of life – there would
be no student debate without the 'key' question. In short, we
discussed everything, starting with the eternal human
problems.

The flowers that I have been sent and the letters I have
received from students who have long since become independent, with families and are no longer young – these are the
most precious presents I have received. In exactly the same
way I value their strict but just opinions of me and of my
work.

I remember very well the first lecture I ever delivered in a
large auditorium. It was when I was still a student in Moscow.
The society called Knowledge arranged for me to deliver a
lecture in a factory club. After the lecture there was to be a
dance – that was the tradition. Quite a large number of people
gathered, mainly young people who, I suppose, had their
minds on the dance. I went up on to the platform and to the
microphone holding my lecture notes.

Were they written on scraps of paper like you are holding now?

Of course not. It was all very proper and thoroughly done.
I looked at the audience and there in the first row I saw an
old man with an enormous grey beard. I can still see him
sitting there! And I took fright. The subject of my lecture was
'Sleep and Dreaming in the Teaching of I. P. Pavlov'. I had
prepared my lecture properly and done a lot of research in the
Lenin Library. But I was apparently conscious of the weak-
nesses in my knowledge of the subject and the theoretical
concepts I set forth. I felt even more vulnerable on account of
my age compared with that of the learned old gentleman who
was, I thought, quite capable of delivering a lecture on the
subject of dreams himself. I read my lecture page by page

without looking up and then waited, terrified, for the reaction. Not from the audience but from the old gentleman, the 'magician'. But, you know, there was complete silence – not a sound, not a single comment. And there wasn't a single question either during the lecture or after it. The old gentleman also remained silent. Apparently everything was absolutely clear to him and to all the others present. Or was he also just waiting impatiently for the dance? But most likely [*she smiled*] the audience sensed what the young lecturer was going through and took pity on her.

I would like to explain to my foreign readers what the Knowledge society is. Its purpose is to spread scientific and political knowledge. And, although I did not make a very good job of the first thing I did for the society, the contact I had with it, lasting many long years, was both useful and very interesting.

Why do you say you did not do well? That there were no questions means you explained everything clearly . . .

I said that I attributed it to the dance. Anyway, when I was in Stavropol I was a member not only of the society's panel of lecturers but also of the presidium of the regional organization. That enabled me to get to know many different representatives of the world of scholarship and art in Stavropol – scholars and poets, writers, actors, doctors, composers, artists and teachers. I knew many of them very well and had frequent meetings with them.

I remember also my first lecture as a teacher at the college. It was in Stavropol at the medical institute, and it was on the history of philosophy. It so happened that on that very day an important commission arrived unexpectedly at the college, officially to 'exchange experience with teachers of social science', but actually to check up on the faculty because of some petty quarrels that had taken place there. The commission included the heads of all the faculties in the town and the best-known social scientists in Stavropol at the time.

And that coincided with your first lecture?

Yes. In fact they had not come to see me but to inspect the college and the faculty. It was quite an important faculty. But the head of the faculty for some reason thought that the best solution was to send the whole commission to visit my class. Although I had only just begun to work at the institute. I was terribly worried!

On the whole I have a good memory. I practically never read my lectures. Only occasionally in the course of explaining the subject I would check my notes for particular quotations, facts and figures. As you know, a lecturer has to work twice – first at his desk, preparing the lecture, which allowed me later to feel completely at ease at the second stage, before the audience. There I could see the faces, hear my students, observe their reaction, if necessary elaborate something, add or repeat something, or reorganize the argument.

But then, when I delivered my first teaching lecture to the students I had absolutely no experience. I had no idea of how much time a given amount of material would take to deliver, how much was needed for a two- or three-hour lecture. I hadn't worked out the ideal rate at which to speak. I had no 'spare' subjects for speaking to the audience if the lecture ended before it was due. That all came later. I forgot to say I had a good attendance – about 200 people. But I finished my first lecture thirty minutes before the bell went. I just didn't know what to do with that half-hour or what to do with myself, to get away from the students and from the commission!

When the lecture was over there was a discussion about it. The commission considered the usual questions. Had the purpose of the lecture been achieved, had the key issues been correctly identified, had the lecture succeeded in establishing the link between philosophy and natural science, and so on.

Suddenly the head of a faculty at the agricultural college asked a question: 'Excuse me, but how long have you been delivering lectures?' I replied, neither alive nor dead: 'This was my first lecture.'

So that you should have a better idea of the situation I will describe to you what I looked like in the face of those venerable professors and the awesome committee. I weighed just fifty kilograms and wore a green dress with a little scarf. You know, during my first years at work I tried always to put on more clothes so as to look more adult and substantial. Even as a child I used to get into trouble with my mother for it. I would put on every piece of clothing I had, and Mama would scold me: 'Now then, what on earth is that? Come on, unpack yourself!' I did the same at college, wearing jackets and sweaters, again in order to look more important, I suppose. It was the fashion at that time for girls to look like women in Deineka's paintings.

'You say it was your first lecture?' The head of the faculty rose. 'Shame on you, colleagues,' he said and left.

The next year he took me on to the staff of his college. He switched to part time himself and suggested that another of the teachers should do the same, and he appointed me to the place he had made. He frequently repeated Khrushchev's remark, very fashionable at the time: 'We are coming back from the fair, comrades.' And he would add: 'And we must help the young specialist.' And he would point jokingly at me. In that way I became a sort of symbolic figure in the faculty – the young specialist – and naturally I tried not to let the head of the faculty down. But he died soon after, unexpectedly.

Do you remember his name?

Of course I do – Nikolai Ivanovich Khvorostukhin. He died of cancer and I soon lost my place in the faculty because of a reduction of staff.

That was a real upset.

A very typical situation, alas. How often something good depends on a single good person!

Throughout my long professional career, frankly speaking, I have never become accustomed to lecturing, in the sense that it never became for me a routine everyday obligation. Every lecture was an examination for me. I was always nervous when I began a lecture, especially before a new audience. Calm and self-confidence came only when I felt that I had made contact, that I had aroused the listeners' interest and held their attention.

Because of the specific nature of the subject I taught – philosophy – and the nature of my research work, which was connected with sociology, the subjects of my lectures were very varied.

I can say without boasting that sometimes women I talk to are surprised at how much knowledge in a variety of fields I have, often in spheres of knowledge very far apart. It is simply because my profession covers such a wide field. The dialectics, for example, presupposes an acquaintance with the natural sciences, physics, chemistry and the general laws of their development. And historical materialism? My work on practical sociology was exceptionally useful for me. Moreover I was not responsible only for student courses. I delivered lectures to graduates and to evening classes attended by mature students with the wisdom of years of experience and with high qualifications and who would not be fobbed off with elementary truisms.

As I said, the subjects of my lectures were very varied: from the history of philosophy, Hegel's *Science of Logic*, Kant on the antinomy of pure reason, Lenin's theory of reflection and of the methods and forms of scientific perception, the problems of consciousness – to the role of the individual in history, the structure and forms of social consciousness, contemporary

sociological concepts, philosophical trends in foreign countries, and so forth.

Of course we were affected by the conditions in the provinces,
the shortage of specialists in the colleges. Efforts to achieve a
narrower specialization in the teaching of philosophy and in the
programmes of public lectures were not successful, mainly
because of the shortage of specialists. You had to be a jack of all
trades. A scholar working in one of the big centres, like Moscow
or Leningrad, usually lectures on only a few subjects – those he
is himself working on. But in a provincial college you are always
being asked to deliver lectures on widely different subjects,
especially if you are young. It is often impossible to persuade
the older lecturers do that, and so they exploit the younger
people. I was one of those they used in this way: apart from my
basic disciplines I taught ethics, the history of atheism and
religion. Not for long, it's true, but I did it. But there was a
bright side to it . . . In the 1960s the Bible, the Gospels and
the Koran appeared in my library, or more precisely in my life
. . . With what difficulty I obtained them! By what strange
routes! But I had them then and it was then that I read them.
And it was then that for the first time I thought seriously about
faith, tolerance, believers and the Church.

An exceptionally important part in my professional career
was played by my interest in sociology. In our country sociology practically ceased to exist as a science somewhere in the
1930s. It turned out – and here too I want to be precise,
because it is important – to be 'unwanted' and perhaps even
'dangerous' in conditions where a bureaucratic command
system was being formed. Sociology is the embodiment of
what we call 'feedback', and for that reason alone a system of
command is organically alien to it. Just as it is alien to the
system.

The revival of sociology began at the very end of the 1950s
and essentially at the beginning of the 1960s. It began slowly,
with difficulty and in contradictory ways. Sociology, a science

dealing with the nature of society, the various forms it takes, what they have in common and how they interact, came up against some very real obstacles in the 1960s and 1970s, against the blind dogmatism of theoretical social thought. Nevertheless many people, including myself, saw sociology as a phenomenon absolutely essential to social thought as a means of overcoming the gap between theory and practice.

Work in sociology opened up for me a whole world of new ideas about society and the names of many talented scholars, philosophers, economists and sociologists both Russian and foreign. It brought me into contact with some remarkable people, the country's leading sociologists, great enthusiasts for their cause, devoted to it and believing in it. They did not have an easy time. It required strength and courage to withstand the resistance to everything new and even its suppression in the 1970s and the early 1980s, in the period later known as the time of stagnation.

Too often sociology tells us rather unpleasant things that don't fit in with the official doctrine.

Yes [*she said thoughtfully*], I consider it very important that I chose the peasantry as the subject of my sociological studies. The Russian village is where we all have our roots and the source of all our strength and perhaps our weakness too. It was important for my development as a young scholar and for my personality and, finally, for the formation of my attitude to life. By no means unimportant also was the fact that my study of the peasantry and its real role was taking place on the basis of material gathered in Stavropol, the region that had been regarded traditionally as an important source of Russia's agricultural production.

At that time we made use of every available means of research to study life in the villages — statistics, all sorts of documents, archives, questionnaires and interviews. You know, I personally collected about 3000 questionnaires in those years. Moreover, I felt that, to a certain extent, I was myself 'inside' the processes and the events taking place in the countryside. I didn't feel like an outsider. On the collective farms I visited the farmworkers' homes, the working brigades, the farms, schools, libraries, shops, medical centres, pre-school nurseries and old people's homes. It was then the first homes for the elderly appeared in our region. In Grigoripolisskoye, for example.

I remember Grigoripolisskoye. It had a children's home. My youngest brother was educated there for a time. I used to visit him. That was also in the 1960s.

You see, it's a small world. I also visited homes for the elderly and have a very good idea of their actual state at the time. I not only visited them: I tried to help them where I could. I delivered lectures and ran discussion evenings. And I had a lot of meetings with the village intelligentsia, most of whom are such selfless people, especially if you bear in mind the conditions they live in and their limited resources.

I also spoke at regional meetings, scientific conferences and seminars, analysing the situation and making recommendations and proposals for the reform or improvement of some aspect of life in the countryside.

The immediate subject of my personal researches which provided the material about which I later wrote my thesis was the peasant family, its material condition, daily life, cultural demands and the nature of relationships in the family. But, along with other researchers from Stavropol and Moscow, I carried out elaborate researches into the region's collective farms — their economics, labour resources, system of wage payments, conditions of life, leisure facilities, and the structure and functioning of the administration.

Not everything went as we wanted it, of course. Nevertheless, I can say without exaggeration that our work acted as a stimulus to the region for other scientists and also for the efforts being made by agricultural specialists, collective and state farm managers. The institute began to receive from various enterprises requests to draw up plans for the social development of working collectives. Our faculty did a great deal in this field, and I know it continued to do this work even after my departure to Moscow.

The sociological researches in which I took part for many years brought me into such close and revealing contact with people and life as I shall never forget. Hundreds of people whom I have questioned on a whole variety of subjects, their recollections, stories and opinions of current events, remain in my memory and are part of my life. I know what their daily life is like and what their problems are. I have travelled hundreds of kilometres along country roads, in a passing car, on a motorcycle or a cart, and sometimes on foot in rubber boots.

A collective farm chairman I know says that a good agronomist always goes around on foot. It doesn't have to be barefoot, he says — times have changed. But he still has to go around on foot. The same is probably true of sociology. It is precisely for the reason that my host did her surveys on foot that her thesis, despite its rather optimistic title — 'The Development of New Features in the Life of the Peasantry in the Collective Farms' — does not stray too far from reality.

As someone once said, in Russia truth still moves in the old way, on foot. Thank God it's not barefoot.

My 'practical sociology' is sociology with a human face, with the faces and the lives that have become part of my life. It has deepened very sharply my conception of 'real life' and my understanding of life and people. And it was in the course of such meetings with real people, and not from books or newspapers, not from plays or films, that I came to understand many of our misfortunes and the questionable nature of many undisputed assertions and established concepts.

It was in the depths of the country that I experienced again the living pain of war, the sad aura of which still enshrouded the nation's life, although it was already twenty years since the war ended. As I conducted comprehensive social surveys of family life I discovered that every fourth or fifth homestead in the villages of the Stavropol region consisted of a single woman. Can you imagine it? A woman who has lost everything, whose life was literally destroyed by war. Of course, I quoted the factual material in lectures and articles, but I hadn't given them enough serious thought, I suppose. More precisely, I didn't perceive the situation as vividly, as visibly or as painfully. But when I came to carry out polls in the villages and every fourth or fifth house turned out to belong to a single woman, then I saw with my own eyes both the homes and the women. Women who had never known the happiness of love or the joy of motherhood. Women living out their lives alone in old, tumbledown houses that were also at the end of their days. If you think about it, we are talking about people whom nature intended to be the givers of life and to be at its centre. And it was amazing to find that the majority of those women had not become bitter, did not hate the whole world and had not withdrawn into themselves, but had preserved the selflessness and the sympathy for the misfortunes and sorrows of others that have always animated the Russian woman's heart. It is really amazing!

Do you think that fate possibly chose you to act on behalf of those women?

'I don't know,' she replied, with a quick glance at me. But I could tell by her look and her reply that that was a subject she did not wish to pursue.

But now that I am alone, sorting out the notes of our conversation, I keep returning to my question. And once again I see in my mind the face of my own mother, who was also left alone by the war, a single mother. How many such women are there whose intended husbands were taken by the world war and by that other war that a poet called 'war with your own people'? There was simply nothing left for them to do but to have children by 'illegal' husbands so as to fulfil their main destiny in the long-suffering Russian land. Illegitimate husbands produce illegitimate children. In my birth certificate, where it asks for the name of my father, there is a blank, while a friend of mine has a sad and eloquent word written — 'illegitimate'.

I would like to believe that the woman I have these conversations with not only was well aware of the fate of such people as my mother but that she will often look with their attentive eyes at the world that is opening up before her.

There is not a scrap of envy in my attitude towards her. Perhaps it is because I now know a little better than others how she feels being at such a dangerous height, the summit of Power. Power and height are the same thing, and to be next to the Power is even more dangerous, because next to the height there is always the neighbouring precipice. Or maybe it is because I am a man and it is, after all, women who are inclined to be more envious of her. I think they will be the main and most 'penetrating' readers of this book. Or perhaps fate has chosen her in the name of all those unknown women who have tragically missed so much that is good and enjoyable in life.

There is something else. I suppose a person who has suffered more feels more sympathy for others? I remember one woman at whose house I turned up late in the evening with my questionnaire, with so many questions to answer. After we had talked and she had answered my probing personal questions she sighed and asked me:

'How is it, daughter, that you're so painfully thin?'

I said, 'Oh no, just my usual weight.'

Still she went on: 'I suppose you haven't got a husband?'

I said, 'Yes I have.'

She sighed. 'I suppose he drinks?'

'No.'

'He beats you up?'

'Certainly not.'

To which she said, 'Come on, daughter, why try to deceive me? I've lived a long time and I know people don't go round from door to door unless they're driven to it.'

Twice, I noticed, Raisa Gorbachev's voice trembled in the course of that long evening: once when she recalled the peasant woman who, after answering the learned questions asked by the young sociologist, began to ask questions herself – very precise and even more down to earth than you find in any questionnaire; and the second time, when she spoke about her daughter. Then I realized that the woman really follows her round the world. She has not faded away.

When I think of my past I often think also of that woman who embodies a great deal for me: the fate of our country, the fate of our village toilers and – and this is also important for me – a sort of national assessment of our sociological activity, which at that time was essentially selfless. 'People don't go round from door to door . . .' – she said then, as though in confirmation of my observations. Yes, it was, after all, a selfless activity which, despite the shortcomings and problems, tried in those years to establish knowledge and truth about life, however unpleasant it might be. As for my thesis, it was partly based on those thousand questionnaires.

Nowadays, in the time of *perestroika*, democratization and *glasnost*, as I observe the development of sociology and the work of sociological services, I wonder if sociology is making full use today of all the possibilities available to it. Is it assisting scientific prognosis and the management of social processes? Or has it again been brought under the control of someone else's subjective will (and it makes no difference whether it is the will of the Government, the Party or the interests of some group) and becoming ever more politicized, departing from objectivity and from the great purpose of all scientific knowledge: to help people and to illuminate and not to obscure the road ahead.

You mean that it is again serving some people rather than the whole of society?

Yes, that is important. There's a need for truth here too. I followed the work of the sociologists' congress: its proceedings were very difficult.

But let's return to talking about our everyday life at that time. Our daughter was growing up. She went to the town nursery and then attended the state school for her general education, the normal local school in our district. She studied music and spent her holidays with her grandparents in the country. We always lived on our own, without the older generation. Our daughter shared with us the joys and sorrows of those years. She helped to keep the house clean, to cook, to do the shopping, and she learned how to make a card-index of our library and even how to arrange my numerous sociological questionnaires and other documents. I must say that my daughter learnt very early in her life to compile a library index. That's a big job in our family because we always had lots of books.

But Irina was only a child, and I constantly had and still have the feeling that at some point in her childhood I did not give her enough attention. I didn't give her as much as I could or, more precisely, as much as she needed. She was born at a time when the law provided for only two months' maternity leave. Our material conditions and our difficulties with employment did not permit me even for a short time to live on my husband's salary. I shall never forget how, early in the morning, I would rush her, only half awake and dressed in a hurry, to the nursery school, almost at the run. And she would keep saying: 'How far away we live! How far away we live!' I shall not forget her little eyes, full of tears and despair, her nose flattened against the glass of the door to the nursery as, when I had been kept late at work, I would again rush into the nursery to collect her. She would cry and keep saying:

'You didn't forget me? You won't leave me?' That's how it was.

Here her voice trembled for the second time.

She was often ill, and quite seriously. We took her to doctors and specialists and obtained various diagnoses and recommendations, often mutually exclusive. That all has an effect on a mother's heart. I tried not to get a doctor's certificate too often, because there was no one at work to replace me. When Irina was older she stayed at home alone. But when she was smaller, I have to admit, I often took her with me to the college. She would sit there playing patiently in the teachers' room and waiting for the end of the working day. People who noticed her as they passed by would ask her questions and she would surprise them with her answers. 'Who do you look like, little one?' 'Like Daddy – the palms of our hands are identical.' 'And what is your name?' 'Zakharenysh.' 'Really? And your mother?' 'Zakharik.'

That was a curious reply.

When I was an eighteen-year-old student I appeared in a photograph and reminded Mikhail Sergeyevich of Zakharka, a figure in a painting by Venetsianov, a Russian nineteenth-century artist. And he began to use that name for me in fun, and so it came to be accepted in our family. Now it has come into use again, with the next generation. Nastenka, our youngest, four-year-old granddaughter, said recently in the presence of some very impressive guests, when Mikhail Sergeyevich asked 'Where is Raisa Maksimovna?' – 'Your Zakharka has gone unstairs.' The guests exchanged surprised glances and laughed. There was nothing for it but to explain who 'Zakharka' was and why the name was used.

In the second class Irina wrote an essay about 'Why I love my Mama'. It turned out to be because I had 'a lot of books' and because 'all the students like Mama because they "say hello to her" and also, most importantly, because "Mama is not afraid of wolves." I still have the essay.'

I see, you are really an ideal archivist.

Perhaps it's a sign of my profession as a sociologist and a lecturer. A sociologist without an archive is like a person without a memory.

Irina was awarded a gold medal on finishing school. In the course of ten years at school she had, as I recall, only one mark less than the highest, and that was for drawing. She finished medical school in the same way, without a single '4'. And I am very proud of that, you know.

In her adolescence and youth my daughter read a great deal, and she admits to me now that she very often used to read into the night 'on the sly'. She says now: 'I appreciated the fact that no one ever told me what I could or could not read or said I was too young to read something. All the books at home were completely at my disposal.' She still likes to read fiction. And some of the things by Tolstoy and Gogol, the short stories of Somerset Maugham, the plays of J. B. Priestley and Margaret Mitchell's novel *Gone with the Wind* were read by her over and over again. I believe she actually knew *Gone with the Wind* by heart.

It's the same with my girls. They talk to each other in the dialogues of Scarlett O'Hara and Rhett Butler.

You know, it's very understandable. Those books contain some strong characters and many fine people. There are wonderful female characters, and male ones as well. And directness and nobility attract the female nature.

I'll take you at your word.

When she was sixteen my daughter and her close fiends acquired their musical idols – Alla Pugacheva, the Beatles, Joe Dassin, Demis Roussos and the musical *Jesus Christ Super-*

star. But Irina tells me now that she prefers the tangos of the 1920s and 1930s. And, like Mikhail Sergeyevich and me, she likes the music of Tchaikovsky, his symphonies and ballet music. She loves Schubert's *Ave Maria*, Leoncavallo's *Pagliacci*, Bellini's *Norma*. The tastes of the generations are getting closer.

In 1974 she began her studies in the Stavropol medical school. In an interview she gave recently to a correspondent of the *Medical News* Irina said that when she finished school she stayed in Stavropol because she did not want to leave her parents. What parent would not be touched by such an admission?

In her first year at the school she got to know her future husband Anatoli. They studied in the same group. Anatoli's mother is a doctor, a neuropathologist. Her father was tall and handsome, devoted to his work as a land surveyor. But he died young of cancer: he was only 56. He suffered a great deal before his death: it is very painful to recall it now. He was operated on twice here in Moscow where we were then living.

Irina and Anatoli were married in 1978, and Anatoli became a member of our family. When I am asked how many children we have I reply 'four' – Irina, Anatoli, Ksenia and Anastasia. But I have brought up one daughter, we had a one-child family. Nowadays they say that a working woman with two children already has enough on her hands. It is not easy to combine professional and public obligations with family duties, with the role of mother and wife.

The right to equal pay for equal work, to material and social independence and to fulfil oneself as an individual – all this represents a tremendous achievement by the women of our day. I have conducted opinion polls among women, asking them whether they would give up their work if their husband was able to provide adequately for the family. Even so, the majority of women replied No.

On the other hand, the family, that social and moral blood

relationship, has always been and remains the most important human institution, the source of people's well-being and happiness or misfortune.

Take for example the actual business of bringing up children. In my opinion our experience demonstrates very convincingly that, with all the tremendous possibilities of social education, and given the evident necessity for it, it is essential that it be combined with a proper upbringing in the family. It is essential! Nothing can replace the emotional, loving relationship between the child and its parents. Not nursery schools or kindergartens or boarding schools or children's homes.

My personal experience of boarding school certainly confirms what you say. Children who have been deprived of parental love, especially those who have been handed over to state institutions, later often, as adults, try to take their revenge on the rest of society for the way they were treated as children.

I believe that, so long as Man himself is fated to exist, the natural feelings of paternal and maternal love will also continue to be experienced. Those same opinion surveys showed that the proportion of women who did not wish to have any children at all was extremely small. How can we reconcile a woman's desire to work and have a profession with her desire to have a family? I suppose that it is today a universal, worldwide problem and a very difficult one to solve. The conditions affecting women's work and its payment, and the state's support of the family, in the Soviet Union, to put it mildly, leave much to be desired.

And if you also take into consideration social conditions in our country, the public services, the health service and the housing situation. And, on top of that, the everlasting shortage of goods. The country now has great difficulties with the supply of foodstuffs and manufactured goods. But as far as I can remember there never were enough of them. For example,

for as long as we lived in Stavropol all our main purchases –
I am not speaking of foodstuffs – were made somewhere else
– in Moscow or Leningrad or on trips abroad. In a word, where
we happened to find things. As soon as a business trip to
Moscow or some similar occasion arose we would start drawing
up a list of our own and our friends' needs. The list would
include everything – books, overcoats, blinds, underwear,
shoes, tights, saucepans, detergents, medicaments . . . You
know how Moscow 'loves' to have all those people descend on
it.

*And even people abroad now know all about our 'lists'. No sooner
do you arrive than they ask you – well, where's your list?*

I can show you a dozen letters from Mikhail Sergeyevich
written, say, from Sochi or from Moscow, saying he has managed to buy some shoes. The never-ending search for things!

Taken together, all these real difficulties result in a situation
where every woman resolves in her own way this problem of
reconciling her professional and family obligations. She sets
out her personal priorities and preferences, moves something
to the foreground and pushes something else to the side. The
result, in my view, is that the scale of values is often upset.

I am sure that the problematical and complicated balancing
of a job and family obligations in our life is one of the reasons
for the lower level of women's professional qualifications and
the slowness of their advance in employment. After all, the
percentage of women with secondary education is not less than
the percentage of men. And there are just as many, even more,
women among students at university as men. But then, as
they advance in years, the women begin to fall behind. Take
the field of science, which I know best. There are, of course,
fewer post-graduates among women scientists than among the
men. Even less have doctorates. And among the living, 'full'
academicians today, how many are women? You can count
them on your fingers.

The situation is exactly the same when it comes to advancing up the ladder of power. At the very top the percentage of women is shamefully small! Despite the fact that there are quite a lot of women among lower-level officials. But as you climb up the hierarchical ladder the percentage of women drops. And it is in no way the laws of nature that are to blame for this but the same imperfections in our society. I have no doubt that they also are partly responsible for the fall in the birth-rate and for the adoption of the idea of the 'one-child family' in our society.

I believe it is not so much the women who are responsible for the tragedy of the voluntary refusal to have any children – and I do regard it as a tragedy. At least it is not only the women who are to blame. Lysistrata, the heroine of Aristophanes's play of that name, who brought a war to an end, is needed in every home. And in every family as a means of preserving it. Because devastating wars can break out in families. But Lysistrata is herself in need of protection and help.

The widespread and, on the whole, very attractive image of the woman as the custodian of the home appears to me today to be something less than ideal. The times demand that woman should play a more active part. Contemporary woman probably has as many roles as she has strength and imagination to fulfil them.

Georgi Vladimirovich, have you seen the statue to Garibaldi in Rome?

I don't recall it.

But I do. There is a statue to Garibaldi in Rome. And do you know who is standing next to Giuseppe Garibaldi in the frieze round the statue? It is Anita Garibaldi, his wife. It is a statue to Garibaldi and, in fact, to Anita Garibaldi, his wife, who accompanied him through all the liberation campaigns and died during one of them. She shared with him equally the ups and downs of his career. She was, after all, a 'custodian of the domestic hearth'.

But let us return to Stavropol. Mikhail Sergeyevich worked in the Komsomol until 1962, when he switched to Party work. As Party organizer he was responsible for the administration of agricultural production on collective and state farms in one of the Stavropol region's districts. Later he became First Secretary of the Stavropol city committee of the Party and then Second and finally First Secretary of the Stavropol regional commitee of the CPSU.

That covered a huge period of time that was very complex and very unusual for the country and the Party. It was a time of hope, but also disappointment. It was the time of the 'thaw', the break-up of many accepted ideas and stereotypes, the development of new ideas and new approaches, and at the same time it was a period when it was impossible to realize fully those ideas and approaches. It was a time for encouraging democratic processes and initiatives and a time that saw the failure of the principal undertakings and reforms and later their complete abandonment.

In April 1958 Mikhail Sergeyevich wrote to me from the 13th Congress of the Komsomol at which Nikita Sergeyevich [Khrushchev] spoke: 'The congress left a very powerful impression . . . conclusions that one does not always arrive at at home . . . vindication for all my worries, strivings and stress . . .' Then something personal: 'I am trying to carry out your requests . . . I'm not going to tell you what I've bought. I'm only sorry I have no more money . . . I have taken out subscriptions for you for a World History – ten volumes – the *Smaller Soviet Encyclopaedia* and Plekhanov's philosophical works . . . I will be back soon, maybe before this letter because there is a possibility I may catch a plane.'

Let us recall in chronological order at least some of the main events that took place from the middle of the 1950s to the middle of the 1970s. February 1956 – 20th Congress of the

Party, Khrushchev's speech, the resolution concerning the 'cult of personality' and ways of overcoming it. October 1956 – the events in Hungary. June 1957 – Plenum of the Central Committee and the resolution concerning the anti-Party group of Malenkov, Kaganovich and Molotov. October 1957 – the launching of the first 'sputnik'. April 1961 – the Soviet space-ship *Vostok* with Yuri Gagarin aboard completed a flight around the Earth. God, how we celebrated then!

October 1964 – the Central Committee of the Party dismissed Nikita Khrushchev as First Secretary and elected Leonid Brezhnev in his place. I have preserved a cutting from the newspaper *Pravda* for the 17th of October 1964. It said in a leading article:

'The Party is the enemy of subjectivism and drift in the construction of Communism . . . The building of Communism is a vital, creative cause. It does not tolerate office-based methods, one-man decisions or a failure to take account of the practical experience of the masses.' What a difference between words and deeds!

March and September 1965 – Central Committee meetings to deal with the situation in agriculture and industry. August 1968 – the events in Czechoslovakia, the introduction of Soviet and allied military units into its territory. 1972 – signing of the first Strategic Arms Limitation Treaty; the world recognizes Soviet nuclear parity with the USA. It was a period that required the rethinking of many fundamental things. Such rethinking does not, of course, come easily. That is why philosophers call the process of acquiring knowledge the 'tortures of Tantalus'.

In the 1960s Mikhail Sergeyevich took a degree in the external faculty of the Stavropol agricultural institute, in the belief that he needed to extend his knowledge of economics to do his work properly. His studies were quite a good addition to his university education as a lawyer and to his civic and professional experience.

As I understand it, you were teaching in the same institute in those years. Were you ever examiner when Mikhail Sergeyevich took a test?

No. I avoided such situations.

Along with his education, something that in my view was very important for his development as a statesman was his entry into the country's ruling circles – the Central Committee of the Party and the Supreme Soviet of the USSR. This opened up for him all sorts of possibilities, including personal contacts with the leaders of the Party and the State.

Raisa Maksimovna, I heard a story that, when Khrushchev visited Stavropol and travelled round the region, Mikhail Sergeyevich was among those who accompanied him and that Nikita Sergeyevich apparently paid him some attention. And gave him his blessing. Is it true?

It's the first time I hear of it. I think it's just a story, except that Khrushchev really did visit the Stavropol region.

What was important was the variety of contacts: not only with leaders of the Party and State but also with his colleagues at the time. Here you had an exchange of useful experience and also of something that was beginning to evoke concern, numerous questions and thoughts and sheer bewilderment. That thought process that went on within himself – believe me – never stopped for a minute. He is not one of those who is ever satisfied with himself or those around him.

In April 1970 Mikhail Sergeyevich was elected First Secretary of the regional committee of the CPSU. He was then, as they used to say, the 'first man in the Stavropol region', a territory comparable with any state in the USA.

Mikhail Sergeyevich's father, Sergei Andreyevich, a peasant who had lived a very tough life, sent a letter on this occasion: 'We congratulate you on your new job. There is no limit to your mother's and father's joy and pride. May that joy never fade. We wish you good health and great strength for your work for the country's well-being.' That very simple letter can still bring tears to my eyes.

I very much regret that Mikhail's father did not live to see his son become Secretary of the Central Committee. It seems to me that his pride in his son would have increased his strength and desire to live.

You dropped the remark that Mikhail Sergeyevich resembles his mother. I would like to correct you – it is not an entirely accurate observation, although you may not agree with me. His facial features are certainly his father's. And his eyes are the eyes of his grandmother Vasyutka. She was his grandmother on his mother's side, the wife of grandfather Pantelei. She was grandma Vasilisa. They all called her Vasyutka, and she had beautiful, bewitching black eyes. Grandma Vasyutka's eyes were handed down to Mikhail Sergeyevich.

Mikhail Sergeyevich and his father were very close to each other and good friends. Sergei Andreyevich did not have a systematic education. He attended classes for the illiterate and went to a school for mechanics. But he had a sort of inborn culture and sense of dignity, and a certain breadth of interest. He was always interested in what Mikhail Sergeyevich was doing and what was going on in the country and the world. When the two of them met he would shower his son with a stream of pointed and vital questions. And his son not only had to answer the questions but also to give account to his father, the peasant and mechanizer. Sergei Andreyevich would listen eagerly and long to what his son said. He died when he was sixty-six, in 1976, just before the 25th Congress of the Party. Mikhail Sergeyevich was already in Moscow but flew back home when he heard his father was very ill. We spent two whole days at the bedside of Sergei Andreyevich, but he did not regain consciousness and we buried him on the 23rd of February 1976.

At this point I will permit myself yet another digression. That portrait of his father faces Gorbachev when he is working in his out-of-town residence near Moscow can also be seen in another place, very far from

Moscow, in the Stavropol region, in the village of Privolnoye in the local village graveyard. On his father's grave is the same image, enlarged from an amateur snapshot and mounted on the tombstone.

So much for Gorbachev's father. As for his mother, you may find the following episode of some interest. I heard of it from my younger brother.

My brother lives in a district not far from Privolnoye and works in the telephone exchange. When the President phones his mother, who still lives in Privolnoye, the call passes through his exchange. One day my brother was instructed by his chief to go down to Privolnoye to see what was wrong with Maria Panteleyevna's telephone, because her son couldn't get through to her.

An hour and a half later my brother arrived at the house, found Maria Panteleyevna and asked her why her telephone was not working. She said that she thought it was working. So why couldn't they get through from Moscow? Then she realized: she hadn't been in the house: she had spent the whole morning working in her garden. The weather was too good to miss!

It was beautiful weather: the end of March, the sun shining, gathering strength awhile, the earth was warming up and a mist was rising from it. The task had been carried out faultlessly and my brother returned to his duties.

The President's mother lives in her village house and cultivates her kitchen garden . . . She lives by her biological, moral or simply peasant time, the natural progress of which is not subject even to the magnetic influence of her son's career. Now say that Russia is a country whose foundations have collapsed. No, we are not just dust in the wind.

Maria Panteleyevna has two sons in Moscow: Mikhail Sergeyevich and Aleksandr Sergeyevich. Aleksandr Sergeyevich was born in 1947, after the war, and is sixteen years younger than his elder brother and is an officer in the Soviet Army.

Mikhail Sergeyevich's election to be First Secretary of the Stavropol regional committee was an unusual move for those days. In the first place, he was a local man. As far as I can remember, the First Secretaries before him were all people from outside the region. They were all 'outsiders'. Incidentally, among the hundreds of congratulations we then received was a letter from the poet Volodya Gneushev. Did you know him?

Of course. He helped me when I was young.

The letter is dated the 14th of April 1970. It also hinted at the fact that Gorbachev was a 'local boy'. The letter read: 'Dear Mikhail! It was only today that a newspaper arrived in Zagedan from which I learnt of your election as First Secretary. I am sincerely glad, not only for you – your election is fully deserved and right – but also for the region which has acquired in you a boss and a friend. That's very good.'

Acquired a boss! The vocabulary of the time.

Perhaps. After all, we are all people of our time. Why deny it? Maria Sergeyevna Larionova, head of the school that Mikhail Sergeyevich attended, also sent congratulations: 'If it were possible, as it was then in the school, when it was announced that the schoolboy Mikhail had been decorated with a medal, to call a meeting, I would like to say to people: "May our region be prosperous. It is now headed by a 'homegrown' secretary of the region who even as a little boy in Privolnoye made the work of a farmer famous throughout the land".'

It would appear that the word 'homegrown' can have a totally positive meaning!

As you see . . . Secondly, Mikhail Sergeyevich was young, just thirty-nine. In those days that was reckoned to be too young for such a position.

Why 'in those days'? Even now there are practically no thirty-

nine-year-olds, not only among party secretaries, but generally among leaders.

That may be. But I would like to read you another message of congratulations from another Stavropol writer, Yevgeni Karpov. He writes: 'Dear Mikhail Sergeyevich! the saying "The egg can't teach the hen" was thought up by stupid, evil and power-hungry people. After all, life itself teaches us that youth means daring, renewal and a fresh wind. Youth is the sunrise, and however wise and beautiful sunsets may be, people still long for the sunrise. It is, of course, far from being just your youth that delights me and my comrades about your election. I send you my heartfelt congratulations and I wish you good, following winds, strong and even stormy ones! Yours . . .'

Although the process was agonizingly slow, nevertheless the pressing need for a renewal of government and Party officials and a change of generations forced its way through. You see, the same people had been in charge everywhere for decades and not only on the district and regional levels but even in the central ruling bodies. In 1978, when the forty-seven-year-old Mikhail Sergeyevich was transferred to work in Moscow, the average age of the members of the Politburo was sixty-seven, and of government ministers sixty-four. The natural process of renewing officials of Party and State, essential for the normal functioning of any society, had been interrupted.

In the few years that Mikhail Sergeyevich worked in the Stavropol region practically all the Secretaries of the local committees were replaced. Along with the appointment of new and younger officials, there was an improvement in the moral atmosphere, there was a new and more dynamic spirit infused into work that embraced not only the Party but all other branches of activity. There was a new spirit and style, characteristic of Mikhail Sergeyevich — frankness, close contact with the people, the ability to listen to and respect other people's opinion, and not to keep down the person working next to you but rather to encourage and support him.

I get the impression that in the course of the last year there has been some change in his manner of communicating with people. Take those 'walk-abouts' in the street. He used to do more speaking himself, heatedly and with enthusiasm. Now he tends more to listen. At such meetings he does not have the look of an orator as he did in the early, romantic days of perestroika, *but rather that of a listener. I see him more frequently in that role, which he probably does not find so easy, given his political temperament. One gets the feeling that, as you put it, there is a great deal going on within him. These changes impress me personally, as does the way he listens patiently to his own people even when the people are clearly 'wrong'. History knows such situations.*

Are you saying that some people have the right to speak, while presidents should mainly listen?

Probably.

He always knew how to listen. He is not only receptive, he is simply 'hygroscopic' in the way he absorbs other people's views. But he acts mostly in the way he thinks necessary.

Is that another privilege of presidents?

Up to a point. You know, even today we are still receiving letters from comrades who worked with Mikhail Sergeyevich at some time. In recalling those years they remember especially and value the fact that, while Mikhail Sergeyevich demanded a lot from them, at the same time he gave them freedom of action – a great deal of freedom.

He once said jokingly in the family circle: 'For me, *perestroika* began in 1970 in the Stavropol region.' His position as First Secretary of the regional committee of the Party gave him the opportunity to achieve something substantial for the region and to put into practice quite a few ideas that had

matured after long and painful debates. It was in those years
that the Stavropol region carried out the intensive development
of new branches of the economy – electronics, power generation and the gas, oil and chemical industries. Tremendous
work was carried out on land improvement in the region,
because Stavropol is, you know, a risky zone for agriculture.
Nearly half the territory of the region consists of steppe lands
subject to drought or of semi-desert. Agricultural production
was reorganized. New ways of organizing the workforce and
providing the people with greater incentives were experi-
mented with. A system of self-financing and piece work was
introduced. It was in those years that the foundations were
laid for truly record harvests in the Stavropol area in the 1980s.
Programmes for the extension of social and cultural facilities
and the reorganization of the region's health resorts were
worked out and to a large extent put into practice. A polytech-
nical institute was opened in Stavropol, as well as a cultural
institute and many secondary technical schools.

*Raisa Maksimovna, I would like to ask you this: It is no secret
that in those years the position of First Secretary of the region was a
very powerful one. The temptation to exercise power was there, not
only for the rulers themselves, but for their wives as well. How did
you feel then in Stavropol in that role?*

The 'temptation' meant for me primarily fresh and never-
ending alarms and worries connected with my husband's work
in addition to my regular professional and family cares. First
came our joint concern, of course, for the affairs of the region.
But our new situation changed our lives to a certain extent
from another point of view: it improved the family's financial
state, provided better opportunities for medical treatment, and
it extended our circle of contacts and acquaintances.

Mikhail Sergeyevich always took his holiday in the autumn
or winter, when all the agricultural work in the region was
over. We took our holidays as a rule 'at home' – in Kislovodsk,

Pyatigorsk or Zheleznovodsk. But when it was possible we
sometimes used our holidays for travelling. We visited Mos-
cow and Leningrad. One year we went to Uzbekistan and saw
Tashkent, Samarkand, Bukhara and the Kyzyl-Kum desert.
Twice in the course of the nine years we went with a group of
Soviet tourists on foreign trips – to Italy and France.

By the time Mikhail Sergeyevich was elected First Secretary
in Stavropol we already had our own separate, comfortable
apartment. But we had to leave it and move into an official
house traditionally occupied by the Secretary of the regional
committee. The question of our move and of whether we ought
or ought not to give up our apartment was not discussed. It
was taken for granted, because the official house had everything necessary for the needs of the region's leader. This was
the beginning of our life in official accommodation.

The next few years turned out to be extremely stressful,
although those preceding it had not been easy, I tell you
frankly: we were both working, continuing our studies and
bringing up a child. And still the nearly nine years that Mikhail Sergeyevich worked as First Secretary were especially tense
for us. Only very rarely were we able to take a holiday or to
have Sunday to ourselves. But when we did get a day off we liked
to spend it outside the town walking through the forests and
steppes. In Stavropol we had no country cottage – neither private nor state-owned. We would put on track suits and cover
fifteen or twenty kilometres on foot. Usually just the two of us,
sometimes with Irina or friends. But the others did not as a rule
want a long walk, preferring a short stroll or a game of volley-
ball. We had so many adventures on our walks, getting lost in
the forest and caught in a blizzard in the steppes. The situation
once took on a dangerous turn, but we were saved by an electric
power line that led us back to the town. Friends had already
raised the alarm, fearing we were lost.

And that was when he was already First Secretary?

Yes. You know, it was so pleasant to be on our own. What a pleasure it is! We would travel out of the town and then go on foot. The forests and the steppes belonged to us. We often got into dangerous situations in the mountains and, I tell you, the most frightening thing is to find yourself in the mountains in a thunderstorm. Then there was an occasion in the forest when some hooligans fired on us. We had reached the depths of the forest when suddenly we heard shots. We had to take cover. There are certainly things to remember.

How did you celebrate the public holidays? There were probably some 'family gatherings' of the region's leaders, at least of the regional secretaries. Stavropolians are a lively lot who enjoy drinking and eating and singing . . .

Of course, we used to get together – for the New Year and the November anniversary of the Revolution. We collected money for it in advance – that was Mikhail Sergeyevich's idea.

We had a great many friends both in Stavropol and in Moscow, and we still have them, both from among colleagues at work and among other folk with whom a single meeting developed into a sincere friendship lasting many years. Among our closest friends are Aleksandr Dmitriyevich and Lidia Aleksandrovna Budyka.

Lidia is a children's doctor with a degree in medicine. As a doctor she helped me to bring up Irina. Her husband Aleksandr is an engineer also with a degree who has risen all the way from being director of a regional tractor station to being a minister in the Soviet government. They are both good and intelligent people who are devoted to each other. They have also been together since their student days. We have been friends with them for thirty years. They have two sons. Mikhail Sergeyevich likes to poke fun at Aleksandr Dmitriyevich: 'Sasha, you're all right but for one fault – you're too much of a liberal.' Budyka always smiles back at him.

Doesn't he call Mikhail Sergeyevich a liberal in return?

No, for some reason he doesn't. Lidia's great weakness is children. A children's doctor by profession, she will go anywhere at any time of the day or night if she can help or save someone. From childhood she has also been very fond of dogs. They always keep one and are always trying to present us with puppies.

For thirty years now we have been friends. Their family has also not been without its sorrows. Lidia's father died young, having suffered the tragedy of false accusations and repressions. Her mother died in great pain. Aleksandr Dmitriyevich's mother is very ill and being looked after by Lidia. Moreover, Sasha himself is a sick man and no longer works. But Lidia, my Lidia, remains the same patient, kindly person she always was. She is such a good and sincere person. I will tell you in simple language: the mere fact that her invalid mother-in-law, who has a daughter of her own, has been living with her for years – that alone tells you something about my friend's character.

In my view, a detail that says everything. The following is an extract from a letter written by Lidia Budyka to the Soviet magazine Peasant Woman *and published in December 1990.*
'There are so many things that come to life in my memory. The lovely, happy years in Stavropol, the walks together, the arguments we had, the games we played, the joyful experiences we went through. But for some reason it is the sadder events that tend to come to mind. That is probably because at the really difficult moments in life a person reveals more true character, exposes things deeply hidden, and so becomes closer and more understandable. That is how it was on that summer's day when Raisa Maksimovna and I flew from Moscow to Krasnodar for the funeral of her father Maksim Andreyevich Titarenko. The previous evening the telephone had rung in our apartment and, after a brief silence, Raisa Maksimovna said, in a controlled and quiet voice: "Lidia, you know, Papa has died."
'I believe that the thousands of pieces of gossip that are spread

around about Raisa Maksimovna are motivated partly by envy and sometimes by hatred but also by the simple, naïve desire people have to believe in the possibility of the existence somewhere or other of an utterly fabulous, carefree, happy life where there are no problems, no bitter disappointments, no illness and no deaths of close friends. But why talk of others when I myself was often deceived when I saw on the television screen her kindly smile and her calm, welcoming manner . . .'

The years passed and changes came about in the life we lived and the people we knew. We also changed. We managed to achieve something, but the problems remained. In the last years we spent in Stavropol I heard Mikhail Sergeyevich speak ever more frequently not only about the difficulties involved in the social development of the villages and towns in the region, the provision of materials and technology, the lack of balance in the terms of exchange of agricultural and industrial output, and the shortcomings in the system of payment for work done. He also talked about the need for profound changes in the country as a whole, in its administrative structure, that were holding up the development of whole regions and particular branches of the economy. He spoke about the difficulties involved in providing the population of the region with foodstuffs and manufactured goods. You see, the region that produced the famous Stavropol wheat, meat and milk and delivered thousands of tons of wool suffered constantly from a shortage of the basic food products and other goods.

In 1978 a full meeting of the Central Committee of the CPSU elected Mikhail Sergeyevich to be a Secretary of the Committee. For both of us it was totally unexpected. Mikhail Sergeyevich was in Moscow and I came home from work late in the evening, about 10 pm. The telephone rang – it was Mikhail Sergeyevich: 'You know, there is an unexpected proposal. There's a Plenum tomorrow. Wait for it. I shall not fail to call you.' On the 27th of November 1978 he became a Secretary of the Central Committee of the CPSU.

You ask me what sort of feelings I had on leaving Stavropol. Was there regret, or was there joy at having at last escaped from the provinces. You know, it's not so simple. Our children really took the move to Moscow as the very height of happiness. Such happiness as, Irina told me later, they did not find in all the years in Moscow. For me the return to Moscow meant the completion of a huge diversion in our lives. It had not been a simple period, nor an easy one, but it is a time I remember fondly. It was there in the Stavropol region that we spent the years of our youth and it was there that our daughter was born and grew up. It was there that we had close friends and family. And it was there, in Stavropol, that we were given the opportunity to realize ourselves.

I was worried once again by that feeling of facing the unknown. I felt rather anxious.

Immediately on our arrival in Moscow we were provided with a country house outside the city. Later we were given an apartment. We obtained accommodation from what was held 'in reserve' and according to what was prescribed in those days for someone with the rank of a Secretary of the Central Committee. Actually it was only later that I understood the rigid system operating in this matter: everything is decided by the unwritten – and, surprisingly, it really is unwritten – Table of Ranks. You will receive only what is laid down according to your position on the hierarchical ladder, and not according to your real contribution to the country's well-being. Alas, the same system operates not only in Moscow but everywhere. Everything depends on the position you occupy and not on the actual contributions you make to the common cause. Just remember my own faculty or any other place of work – you get paid according to your position, and that's that. Position stood for everything and still does. Initiative, creativity and independence, not only in big things but in the smallest everyday matters, were not encouraged, or not encouraged very much.

In accordance with the accepted rules high officials in ministries and government departments and also those in the headquarters of the Central Committee of the Party were provided
with country houses in special areas belonging to those organizations. The top political leadership – Members and Candidate Members of the Politburo and Secretaries of the Central
Committee – lived in protected government dachas situated
in the suburbs. Their houses were provided with servants and
equipped both for relaxation and for work, and they were
provided free of charge so long as the occupant kept his
position.

Similar houses in Moscow and other places were used for
entertaining important foreign guests and other represen-
tational purposes. And there was accommodation in the
country's health resorts set aside for Soviet leaders and leaders
of foreign states.

There is one other detail I would like to mention. Among
the Party and government officials with whom I had come into
contact in previous years the building of one's own private
dacha was considered to be quite impermissible. Responsible
officials in the Stavropol region had neither state-owned nor
private dachas. They could have a plot of land for a garden if
they wished, but they could not build on it.

When we found ourselves in Moscow in 1978 one of my
many discoveries was that, it appeared, some members of the
country's leadership, including Party leaders, who already had
dachas provided by the State, were also building their own
private dachas, for their children, grandchildren and so forth.
I was struck by such economic enterprise and daring.

We were put first of all in an old wooden cottage which
had been occupied in its day by Sergo Ordzhonikidze and was
in need of a major overhaul. After two years we were given a
different one, a new, brick-built house put up in the 1970s.
Before us it was occupied by F. D. Kulakov. In 1985, after
Mikhail Sergeyevich's election as General Secretary of the

Party, we moved to a new house that had all the conditions, facilities and means of communication necessary for him to carry out the functions he was entrusted with. That is where we are now, in Mikhail Sergeyevich's study. The one we left was taken over by Boris Yeltsin, who was then Secretary of the Moscow city Party and had just become a Candidate Member of the Politburo. As far as I know, he continued to occupy it until he gave up Party work.

In our last years in Stavropol our monthly family income consisted of the 600 roubles Mikhail Sergeyevich was paid as Secretary of the regional committee plus the 320 roubles I was paid as a lecturer. It was on the whole a good income for those days. As a Secretary of the Central Committee Mikhail Sergeyevich was paid 800 roubles a month. If I am not mistaken, all the Secretaries, Candidate Members and Members of the Politburo and the General Secretary received the same. Apart from that there were additional monthly payments 'for food' – 200 roubles a month for Secretaries and Candidate Members and 400 roubles for full Members of the Politburo.

We were permitted to acquire essential books free of charge. Not only the head of the family but his wife too was provided with free transport in the form of a car and chauffeur. The apartment was rent-free and a sum of money was allotted to pay for holidays. In recent years, all these privileges, including the use of state-owned country houses, have been withdrawn.

In accordance with decisions taken by the Congress of People's Deputies of the USSR, the Supreme Soviet passed a Resolution 'Concerning the remuneration, servicing and protection of the President of the USSR', and of the Chairman of the Supreme Soviet, the Vice-President and the Prime Minister. The President of the USSR was allotted a salary of 4000 roubles a month. Taking into account the current level of taxes and other payments that means a 'take-home' pay of 2500 roubles. He is provided with residences in the Moscow area and in the Crimea, an official apartment in Moscow, the necessary transport facilities and a specially equipped plane and helicopter. On his retirement the President of the USSR receives a pension for life amounting to 1500 roubles a month, is provided with a state-owned dacha with the necessary staff, bodyguard and transport. So much for the material aspects.

When I come to recall 1978 I remember that the move to Moscow meant for me new professional opportunities, visits to my favourite theatres, concert halls and exhibitions, and meeting actors and musicians whom we met previously only occasionally when we were in Moscow.

Irina and Anatoli transferred to the Second Medical Institute. Both of them passed out with distinction and in 1985 Irina presented her thesis on problems of medicine and demography. She worked initially as an assistant in the faculty of social hygiene and organization of the health service at the Second Moscow Medical Institute. Later she took up scientific research and joined the laboratory for medical–demographic and sociological research. Anatoli also took a degree in medicine as a surgeon. He has been working for more than ten years in the Moscow city clinical hospital.

A year after our arrival in Moscow our first real Muscovite – our granddaughter Ksenia – was born. We decided on her name before her birth. I chose it – they trusted me. The second real Muscovite, granddaughter Anastasia, was born in 1987. Her name was chosen collectively by the whole family. Mikhail Sergeyevich's proposal won the day, so that in that respect we are on equal terms. Actually they twice prepared a masculine name – in case it was a boy. Then it would have been Mikhail.

But all that is about the joys of family life. There were other things too. To say that we found ourselves in Moscow in a new and unfamiliar environment and atmosphere is really to say very little or even nothing at all. I will not take it upon myself to judge the atmosphere and the kind of relations there were among the leaders, Mikhail Sergeyevich's colleagues. I rely only on my own experience and my personal impressions, mostly of the members of the families of the Soviet leaders at the time.

The first thing that struck was the way people were estranged from one another. Whether you exist or not, whether you existed in the past or not was not to be gathered from the faces surrounding you. You were seen and somehow not noticed. Even the usual greetings were not exchanged. There was surprise if you addressed someone by his or her first name and patronymic. What? – you actually remember them? In company people often displayed pretensions to superiority, to being one of the chosen. Judgements were pronounced categorically and often without tact.

What struck me about relations between members of a family was the mirror image they provided of the same respect for rank as existed among the leaders themselves. I remember how once I wondered aloud about the behaviour of a group of young people. The woman I was talking to was very upset and exclaimed: 'What are you saying –. that's Brezhnev's grandchildren there!'

We women used to meet mainly at official occasions and receptions, and only seldom privately. But even when we met in a small circle of friends the same rules of the 'political game' operated. There would be endless toasts to the health of those higher up, nasty talk about those lower down, discussion of food and about their children's and grandchildren's 'unique' abilities. And card games. I was struck by the evidence of indifference and lack of concern. Could I call it 'consumerism'? For example, at one of the gatherings at a state dacha I warned the children: 'Be careful, you'll break the chandelier!' In reply I was told: 'Not to worry. It's government property, it can be written off.'

The children replied like that?

The grown-ups . . .

I remember the reaction to a trip that Mikhail Sergeyevich made to England in 1984 at the head of a parliamentary delegation. With Konstantin Chernenko's permission I travelled with him. The delegation's trip turned out to be extremely interesting, substantive and productive of good results. It was reported in our press but more fully in British and American publications. When I returned home I heard people say: 'Why did they sing your praises so highly over there? Don't you realize what it all means? What have you done to attract the West? Now then, now then, let's look a bit closer at you . . .'

Turn round, young man?

More or less. Formalism and callousness penetrated even amongst the service staff. I always had warm but sad feelings when I recalled people who worked for us previously. Our chauffeur Anatoli Andreyevich Khamukha was demobilized from the army and worked for Mikhail Sergeyevich in Stavropol for twenty years. I knew his wife and his children and we still exchange greetings on national holidays.

Mikhail Sergeyevich's hopes that here, at 'the top', he would be able to solve some pressing problems were not realized in many respects. Our troubles were driven inwards and postponed for the future. Leonid Ilich Brezhnev was a sick man and that had an effect on everything. In November 1982 he died. Then came the turn of Yuri Vladimirovich Andropov. But the hopes that were aroused proved not to be long lived. Andropov was seriously ill. It's an awful thing to recall, but at his funeral I saw some openly happy faces.

Then came the time for Konstantin Ustinovich Chernenko. That period was even more complicated. The country was living in hope of changes, the need for which was felt everywhere. The number of people was increasing who openly supported and understood the necessity of ideas about reform and the practical steps needed to bring them about. But everything remained as it was in the life of the Party and of the country. Mikhail Sergeyevich and I would discuss things at length after he returned from work. We talked about a lot of things — about the same things as were being discussed in society with increasing concern and insistence.

There's another matter that suddenly came to mind, Georgi Vladimirovich. There are people, I know, who are interested in the external side of my life. They even envy me — for the clothes I wear and my 'apparel' on formal occasions . . . But I value something quite different — my participation in the tremendous undertakings that have fallen to the lot of someone close to me — my husband.

Never before had we talked at such length — six half-hour reels had been used up and a seventh was half used. A pile of prepared notes we had gone through lay on the desk next to Raisa Maksimovna. Since the pieces of paper were of all shapes and sizes the pile reminded one more of a Chinese pagoda with turned up edges . . . One can tell that she is tired, and who wouldn't be after several hours of such work?

I had also prepared some photographs [*she said, pointing to a fat, well-packed envelope at the end of the sofa*]. But we probably won't look at them today, it's too late. Next time, yes?

You know, I would quite like to look at them now, just to glance through them quickly. It's interesting. {I risked seeming to be impolite.}

Very well. Have a look at them on your own. I'll be back shortly.

She handed me the envelope, or rather the packet, and went into the other room, the library.

For some time I sat there alone, glancing through the photos in the packet. The Stavropol house I already knew. The students from the agriculture institute gathering corn. In sports clothes the young teacher is indistinguishable from the girl students. Gathering mushrooms somewhere in the foothills of the Caucasus. Then Moscow. Meetings with lots of people, airports. Boris Yeltsin, who took over their dacha, handing Raisa Gorbachev a few carnations with a very elegant and polite bow. Strange but true!

Somewhere, in Roy Medvedev's book, I think, I read a story that four leaders of the USSR once met on the platform of the railway station at Mineralnye Vody. One, Brezhnev, was still active as General Secretary — in so far as he could be called 'active' at that time. And there were three future General Secretaries — Chernenko, Andropov and Gorbachev. Brezhnev and Chernenko were said to be travelling from the south and the sea. Andropov was holidaying in Kislovodsk. Gorbachev had naturally travelled from Stavropol for such an occasion. The platform is said to have been cleaned up and cordoned off, and the four men paced slowly up and down the empty platform on that late autumn evening beneath the dim, also rather autumnal, lamps. Like Russia, the long train waited for the signal to start moving.

I know the station platforms at Mineralnye Vody too well to forget that story as I looked through the old photographs. But no such photograph did I find in the packet, and I would certainly have recognized that platform.

All the same, there was a photograph of a platform. It was faded, just an amateur snapshot, but quite distinct. In the foreground was a young, laughing woman in velvet jeans, with dimples on her cheeks and a shock of dark, chestnut hair blowing in the wind.

That was our first time in Paris as tourists. We had only just stepped off the train [*she explained, glancing over my shoulder*].

Her husband, I realize, was not to be seen: he was handling the camera. It was the only photograph taken of her in Paris at the time. Moscow was still ahead. Paris too, like Washington, Bonn and Madrid . . .

When I proposed to devote one of the chapters of the future book to happiness and call it accordingly 'About Happiness', she thought a little and then turned the idea down:

Do you really think, Georgi Vladimirovich, that I resemble a woman flitting from happiness to happiness?

No, she doesn't — I see that now more clearly. All the same, that woman on the empty platform had more than a laughing face — she seemed to me to be happy.

But the state of happiness, they say, lasts only for minutes. All the rest is just life.

CHAPTER FIVE

Things I Take to Heart

Everything was the same as before in the President's study with one exception: there was a pile of letters, telegrams and postcards lying on the leather divan. A few days previously the President had celebrated his sixtieth birthday.

I am sorting them out [*Raisa Maksimovna said*]. We have already counted more than 3000 letters and telegrams. Would you like to see the present Russian Patriarch Aleksi II sent for the occasion?

Yes, I said. We went into the library, where I was shown an ikon in a beautiful setting decorated in gold leaf. The Archangel Mikhail peered out sadly and severely from behind the glass of the icon case. He looks rather sad, I said.

It would be strange if the guardian angel looked otherwise.

She then showed me a tiny ornament in the lacework.

Archistratig. The sign of the supreme leader of the heavenly host.

We stood there, admiring the ikon. It was a dull day, but the ikon seemed to gather together and focus all the light dispersed in the room and shone softly in the depths of the library. I then remembered that it would soon be Easter.
I saw on a desk nearby two piles of books, both more than a foot high. What was on the top today? What are they reading now? An elegantly bound volume – Love Songs – poetry – frankly, something

I had not expected — and on the other pile a volume of Pushkin. It was a blue, rather faded volume from the ten-volume edition issued in the 1950s. I opened it at the bookmark — Boris Godunov.

That's what I am reading [*she said from behind my back and took the open book from me*]. 'I feel there's nothing can reassure us / midst all our worldly cares / Nothing, except maybe our conscience: / if it is clear it will triumph / over malice and wicked slander.'

She read quietly, as though to herself, and then closed the book and placed it next to the ikon. The Archangel Mikhail and the profile of Pushkin stamped on the book cover seemed to make quite natural neighbours. A minute later our final conversation was under way.

Where shall we start? [*she asked, without waiting for a question*]. Konstantin Ustinovich Chernenko died on the evening of the 10th of March 1985. Nothing had been revealed concerning his condition and illness. On the 2nd of March came the results of the elections to the republican Supreme Soviets. They showed that 99.98 per cent of the electors had turned out to vote, and that over 99 per cent of them had voted for the nominated candidates.

What figures! How quickly we have changed our ways.

That we have done so is all for the better, I think. Chernenko was elected as a Deputy to the Supreme Soviet of the Russian Federation. The press reported that the electoral commission had handed him the certificate confirming his election, and his address to his constituents and the Soviet people was published. But there was not a word about the fact that Konstantin Ustinovich was in hospital and very gravely ill.

Moreover, on the 6th of March, in accordance with a long-standing practice in our country, his wife Anna Dmitrievna gave a reception on the occasion of International Women's Day. It is given for the wives of the heads of foreign diplomatic missions accredited in Moscow. As was the custom, the reception included dances, songs and a concert.

When Chernenko died Mikhail Sergeyevich was informed immediately, and he called an urgent meeting of the Members and Candidate Members of the Politburo and the Secretaries of the Central Committee. Decisions were taken regarding the funeral. An emergency meeting of the Central Committee was called for the next day, and at that meeting on the 11th of March Mikhail Sergeyevich was elected General Secretary of the Party Central Committee. A great deal has been written about those meetings of the Politburo and the Central Committee. All sorts of points of view, conjectures and opinions have been voiced. According to what Mikhail Sergeyevich told me, neither in the Politburo nor in the Central Committee were any other candidates put forward for the post of General Secretary. By that time the majority of the members of the Central Committee had probably arrived at a common point of view in their assessment of the situation that had arisen both in the leadership and in the country as a whole. It was a very difficult, complex situation of internal tension. Outwardly everything looked normal. Mikhail Sergeyevich's election was unanimous.

It was late when he returned home. The whole family was there to meet him with flowers. Ksenia, who was then only five, said: 'Grandpa, I congratulate you. I wish you happiness and that you will eat up your porridge.' Mikhail Sergeyevich laughed and asked: 'And will you eat it along with me?' 'No! My muscles are tired of chewing it.' 'But you must,' said Mikhail Sergeyevich, laughing. 'I don't like it either, but, you know, I eat it, I have to . . .'

We grown-ups congratulated Mikhail Sergeyevich and were happy and proud of him and had confidence in him.

But on that evening, of course, neither the children nor I had any real idea of the burden that he had taken upon himself. We couldn't imagine a hundredth part of what Mikhail

Sergeyevich's 'new job' was going to mean in reality or what awaited him and all our family in the future.

You, Georgi Vladimirovich, will probably want to ask: if I had known then that everything would be so complicated and so full of drama, would I not have tried to dissuade Mikhail Sergeyevich?

That is a question.

Now I want to reply to it in complete sincerity. Despite the burden of what we are going through today, I am not going to say Yes in haste. No, I cannot say it. We did not, of course, know that things would be as they are today. But tell me – Do you not ask yourself today: what would it have meant for the country and the people if then, in 1985, someone much the same as his predecessors had come to power and, what is more, would remain there for another fifteen years or so? How would that have ended up? What kind of situation in the country would we be talking about today – if we were actually talking at all? Where would that have led the country? Six years ago that was what we thought about in the first place. That was why Mikhail Sergeyevich made such a decision.

A month later, in April, there was a full meeting of the Central Committee at which Mikhail Sergeyevich made a major speech. The Committee passed a resolution calling for the regular congress of the Party to be held in February 1986. That meeting, known as the April Plenum, is now regarded as the turning point. But we still had ahead of us the 27th Congress of the Party, the Nineteenth nationwide Party conference and the First Congress of People's Deputies of the USSR.

In 1985 Mikhail Sergeyevich made his first trips round the country – in May to Leningrad, in June to Kiev, Dnepropetrovsk, in July to Minsk, and in September to the Tyumen and Tselinograd districts. This later became a regular part of his work, and not only for him but for all the country's leaders. In that way new traditions came into being. But then it was something unusual and new. And those encounters with the people were not just for show: they were frank, and by no means always very pleasant, but always very sincere conversations about everything that was worrying people. They were heart-to-heart talks, sincere and concerned.

He acted similarly when he went abroad.

Yes, but that was later.

The hour-long speech that Mikhail Sergeyevich delivered on the 17th of May in the Smolny Institute in Leningrad was also broadcast by television, which was regarded as something extremely unusual. In the first place Mikhail Sergeyevich did not read off a prepared speech, but spoke naturally, reasoning and explaining his personal understanding of the serious problems in the economy. He was consulting with the people. And, secondly, he was addressing the whole country, all the Soviet people, at once. Never before − with a rare exception − had speeches by leaders of the Party and the country at Party conferences, congresses and groups of activists been broadcast by television, and, what's more, transmitted 'live'.

It must be said that the country reacted very quickly to these innovations. Remember those political jokes that went around?

You mean to say you heard them?

Of course − both those and some of the contemporary 'folklore'. For example, I recall one of the jokes going the rounds in 1985: a man living in the far north returns from Moscow and is asked: 'Well, how are things there at the centre, do they support Gorbachev?' 'No, they don't support him.' 'Really?' 'No, they don't support him. Can you believe it − he walks without any support.' And here's another wisecrack: 'This Gorbachev is quite illiterate.' 'How can you say that when they say he's got two degrees?' 'All the same, he's illiterate. All the ones before him read their speeches, but he just talks . . .'

In that same year, 1985, the General Secretary carried out official visits to France, Poland, Bulgaria and Czechoslovakia. In November he had his first meeting with the President of the United States of America, Ronald Reagan, in Geneva. Before he visited France, for the first time in our country's history, the leader of the Party and of the State talked with foreign, Western journalists on the television. That had previously been unthinkable.

Also in 1985 there was the first official visit to our country of the head of a foreign government since Mikhail Sergeyevich became General Secretary. It was the visit of Mr Rajiv Gandhi. In accordance with the protocol the ceremony of greeting the distinguished guest began at the airport and was due to end on one of the big squares within the Kremlin walls. But it rained that day. The very moment the cars drove into the Kremlin it simply came down in torrents. We who were there to welcome Gandhi had to take cover against the buildings . . . Rajiv and Sonia Gandhi had to shoot out of the car and dash across to us beneath an archway. They were young, handsome and full of strength and optimism in the midst of a Russian downpour.

It meant good luck?

I hope so. Years later I was able fully to appreciate something else – their genuine civic courage.* Incidentally, changes were later made in our diplomatic protocol for greeting and seeing off the heads of foreign states and governments.

---

* This book was already in production when on the 21st of May 1991 came the terrible news of the murder of Rajiv Gandhi. It literally stunned Mikhail Sergeyevich and me, and we sent a telegram of condolence to Mrs Sonia Gandhi in which we said that Rajiv Gandhi was our great personal friend and that we fully shared her inconsolable grief.

I would like to add to that personal message only one thing: that Rajiv Gandhi was not only our personal friend – he was a great friend of our whole people, and the news of his tragic death was received with sadness in every Soviet home.

The ceremony for receiving guests by the Chairman of the Presidium of the Supreme Soviet of the USSR and later the President of the country no longer takes place on a square in the Kremlin but in the St George's Hall of the Great Kremlin Palace.

Six years ago Mikhail Sergeyevich and those who shared his views initiated some reforms which came to be known throughout the world as *perestroika*. The reforms were aimed at finding new paths for the development of our country's domestic and international policy, in the conditions of a new period and a new existence for our common human home.

The agenda included economic and political reforms, the replacement of the old and obsolete organization of the administration and the bureaucracy, and the establishment of a state governed by the rule of law. The conception of new thinking in international relations meant, as I understand it, the recognition of the priority of political means over the use of force, non-interference in other countries' affairs, and the prevention of a nuclear or ecological catastrophe on a world scale.

As I listed all that, Georgi Vladimirovich, I was thinking that nowadays for us and for many, many people in our country and beyond it such a programme sounds like something quite ordinary. We are used to that. But, you know, behind every statement, every sentence and every thought there is the agonizing process of rethinking and reassessing the past. **Truly agonizing!** It has been the most difficult search for answers to questions and problems that time has faced us with so urgently and imperatively. And what a struggle it has involved, internally, but not only internally. It is still going on.

I was a witness of how, during the drafting of the report to the Party's 27th Congress and in the course of the most heated discussions between Mikhail Sergeyevich's closest collaborators, there emerged new ideas about the contemporary world, regarding it as a single civilization with all its contradictions and problems. At that time Mikhail Sergeyevich said in the

Central Committee's report to the Congress in February 1986:

'The course of history and social progress is demanding ever more insistently the establishment of constructive and creative cooperation between states and peoples on the scale of the whole planet . . . Such cooperation is necessary in order to avoid a nuclear catastrophe so that civilization may survive . . . That is the way, through a conflict of opposites, with great difficulty and to a certain extent just feeling our way, that a contradictory, mutually dependent and in many ways single world is evolving.' In 1986, such statements amounted to a revolution!

The ideas behind *perestroika* and the steps taken to bring them about turned out from the outset to be attractive to people and were eagerly seized upon by them. The solidarity and support in the feelings, the words and finally in the eyes of hundreds of thousands of people who came out to welcome Mikhail Sergeyevich on his trips around the country and abroad, became the emotional background of *perestroika*. Support and unity was to be seen in the continuous stream of letters. In 1985 Mikhail Sergeyevich received up to 40,000 personal letters a month. Altogether in 1985 he received 402,500 letters! And those were, I repeat, only the personal ones and not the letters addressed generally to the Central Committee. In 1986 Mikhail Sergeyevich received over 60,000 letters a month, again personal ones. In 1990 he received up to 40,000 letters a month and in January and February 1991 93,000.

I am convinced that there is no more accurate, more revealing or more honest document relating to the *perestroika* period than those letters. The letters contain a history of *perestroika*, an analysis of the ideas behind it, advice, suggestions, reflections, all the tension and drama of *perestroika*. There is no point in concealing the fact that there were also letters full of malice, of hatred and of rage. But the majority were letters of support, of hope and of determination to act.

I would like, of course, to read a few of the letters, or at least some extracts. 'Perestroika is what the people long for. Do not stray from the path you have chosen, do not retreat – A. Lavrik, Svobodny, Amur region.' 'If there is a return to the past then better the hangman's noose' – that was in a letter from L. Sheveleva in Bratsk. 'We have faith and hope – A. Feklisov, Moscow.' 'Please take care of your health: the battle is just starting – E. Glushkov. Yuzhno-Sakhalinsk.' 'It is clear to everybody how much of your energy, time, intellectual strength and health is being consumed by the colossal, inhuman burden you have brought down upon yourself. It is always difficult to build . . . Perhaps it will be a little easier for you if you know that the huge mass of ordinary people are entirely behind you, that they admire you and support you – K. Lasta. Leningrad.' 'God grant you great victories, you great and dear person. Mikhailina – Rovengan, Ukraine.' 'Dear Mikhail Sergeyevich. Dear man! I am not too shy to address you with that word because you are close to all honest people – Chermak family, Chernovtsy.'

'I am endlessly proud of you as I observe your efforts abroad. Mikhail Sergeyevich, the cause of peace is the most important thing for all of us. If necessary all of us ordinary folk are ready to give up everything and to live on bread and water if only we can preserve the peace. I beg you to guard your health. You have totally conquered the love and gratitude of our people – Z. Potop. Kyshtym.'

This letter I want to quote in its entirety:

'You know, it has become interesting to be alive . . . Previously I didn't pay much attention to what was being said on the television. And I must admit I wasn't very interested in reports of congresses and plenums. It seemed to be going on far away from me and hadn't much to do with me. But now, whenever you speak on the television I demand absolute quiet at home. I always watch the programmes with tremendous interest and read the reports of your meetings with workers

and collective farmers. If there is something I don't understand
I read it again. Now I even regret not becoming a member of
the Communist Party. Just as, incidentally, I regret that we
have only one girl. You know, there was constant fear for the
future – what if war broke out tomorrow? Now I look to the
future with hope and think: it is impossible that a man should
make such an effort and so many peace proposals and not
succeed in ridding us all of the madness of nuclear war . . . I
have written you this letter so that you should know that we
workers are with you heart and soul. There has been so much
to understand and think about in the last year that I just
couldn't fail to share with you my feelings and thoughts –
L. Bardetskaya. Kirov region.'

Here's another one. 'Hold on, right is on your side. My
letter may be just a drop in an endless ocean, but I very much
want to thank you, to support you and beg you never to retire.'
The writer is, as you see, a maximalist – 'never'. He continues:
'You may sometimes lose heart on account of what is going
on in the world. But don't give up, because right is on your
side and your initiatives serve the interests of the whole world.
Thank you for your courage. Thank you – M. J. Lelotte.
Belgium.'

Here are the very recent letters: One from S. Gersh in
Yuzhno-Sakhalinsk: 'I want very much simply to voice my
support in a friendly way for your efforts to bring about *perestroika*, and to let you know that we have faith in you and your
undertakings. In Sakhalin we have detected at least a glimmer
of light, a little hope for a better future. So I beg you to carry
through to the end the cause you have started, however difficult it may be.'

This one is from A. Aborvanov, a professional driver from
the village of Donskoye in the Orenburg district. 'I and the
people who elected me greet you warmly and support you. To
have supported the Church and at the same time to have
awakened the people you have aroused a feeling of goodness

and of mutual understanding in people which we so lacked in the period of stagnation. I advise you as a friend to keep to the course you have indicated and which will lead our country into the future. Good health and strength and long life to you. May this letter give you more strength and confidence. I believe the support of the people is a good platform from which to perform good deeds.'

Here is a letter dated the 6th of March 1990 from O. Turkina, who is an engineer in the Novolipetsk metallurgical complex. It is signed by her, her husband S. Turkin, and her sons Dima and Misha Turkin.

Greetings, dear Mikhail Sergeyevich!

I wanted to write this letter to you a year ago but had no hope that you would ever read it. Perhaps today you are in need of support and my letter will give you encouragement. A year ago a second son was born to us and we called him Mikhail Sergeyevich in your honour (my husband's name is Sergei). I am 34. I am not a member of the party and I work as an engineer in the Central Heating Laboratory at the Novolipetsk metallurgical complex. From the first year of *perestroika* I have been your ardent supporter. Having called my son Misha (everybody knows it was in your honour) I have linked my fate closely with yours. I suffer badly when there are setbacks in this period and I rejoice at the successes. It is painful to hear the avalanche of attacks on your good name. I have faith in you, in our country's future and in our people. I would be very glad to learn that you have read this letter . . .

The ideas of *perestroika* captured the emotions and imagination of many members of the artistic intelligentsia. Their support and their inspired words were of tremendous significance in enabling society to understand the aims of *perestroika*. Do you recall the poem Yevgeni Yevtushenko wrote in 1988, in which he used Mikhail Sergeyevich's remark that 'we can't go on like this' as a sort of refrain?

> When our country almost went off the rails
> We kept it on by the skin of our teeth
> And realized as we held it back:
> 'We can't go on like this!'

In the last few years many authors have sent us signed copies of their books in which much of importance and significance has been said.

We take great care of letters received from scholars, authors, cinema people and publicists. In reply to a note I sent to Tatyana Ilinichna Ivanovna about an article she wrote in *New Times*, she wrote me the following in 1990:

> . . . Thank you for your kind words. Believe me, if I could and knew how to, I would do something very good for you. And, of course, for Mikhail Sergeyevich. But I can't think of anything. I would so like to give you some pleasure . . . In return for all the happiness that many (very many, you know) like me have experienced in the course of these last five years. My God, it is customary to say that youth is the happiest time of your life. But I am forty-seven and my happiest years began just five years ago. Moreover, it is a rather special kind of happiness – freedom and dignity are its main features. Gorbachev is a great man. Great and wonderful. Take his meeting with the young people – once again I admired the replies he gave. I am proud that I have such a President. I can very well imagine (as it seems to me) the impossible load on his shoulders and yours.
>
> I do the best I can. May you both be protected by fate, the heavens or God, if after all he exists. Keep well and

young as long as you can. If people like me (and our
number is legion) had risen from our seats along with
the delegates to the Third Congress to greet Gorbachev
on his election to the post of President, believe me – and
let him know this – the world has never heard such
ovations as he would have heard from us. I congratulate
you, Raisa Maksimovna and Mikhail Sergeyevich, on the
spring holidays. And on the best of them – the birth
of *perestroika* especially. Thank you once again . . .

N. A. Benois, the grandson of Nikolai Benois, and a remarkable Russian artist, representative of a famous artistic family
that has done so much for Russian culture, wrote me from
Italy on the 23rd of February 1988:

Dear Raisa Maksimovna!
   I beg you to forgive me for permitting myself to address
these lines to you although I do not have the pleasure
or the honour of knowing you personally. But I have long
had the intention of expressing to you and your brilliant
husband the unlimited admiration we experience over the
grandiose nature of *perestroika* . . . in the field of the
domestic and foreign policy of our vast and, in all senses,
great Soviet Union, thanks to which the whole structure
of Soviet life will be radically renewed (and, I would say,
rejuvenated) in accordance with Lenin's guidelines. So
the true paths for the achievement of genuine socialism
will be established. So permit me, dear Raisa
Maksimovna, to express to you, since I have at last dared
to write to you, my great admiration for the grandiose
historical initiative upon which the ultimate fate of the
great Soviet country will depend. And I wish from the
bottom of my heart that you and our respected Mikhail
Sergeyevich will be able successfully to perform further
work for the good of humanity. But the purpose of this

letter consists not only of my fervent desire to convey to
you and your remarkable husband my feelings, but also
to thank you from the bottom of my heart for the
interest and attention which you have shown in the
creation of the Benois family museum: in Petrodvorets on
the outskirts of heroic Leningrad, birthplace of practically
all the members of the 'creative part' of our vast artistic
family . . .

Perestroika is all the time extending its front, digging in and
embracing one new sphere after another. As a person, as a
citizen, in view of my personal conviction, I could not, of
course, remain aside from its development. But for me it
meant primarily to be at Mikhail Sergeyevich's side, to help
him and support him as far as my strength and abilities permitted.

*Raisa Maksimovna, I keep wanting to ask you: what about your
own work? Did it occur to you, let us say, to complete your doctoral
thesis?*

Yes, it did. But I had ceased to be engaged in my own
professional work. I won't say that it was a simple or easy
thing to do. On the contrary I agonized over it. For some time
I continued to gather material for the doctoral thesis and
attended philosophical seminars and conferences that interested me. I continued to follow the philosophical and sociological literature that was published, and I maintained active
contact with my colleagues. But the circumstances of my daily
life faced me with a choice and I made that choice. Other
people can write doctoral theses . . .

*But you are contradicting yourself. Last time you were arguing in
favour of women playing a more important role in science and for
intellectual equality.*

Quite so. But everything in life is specific. Remember: 'the truth is always specific'. Today I do not regret the choice I made. It was what my family and I needed most. The position of lecturer in the faculty of philosophy remains the last position I held officially in my life. But, to be completely honest, I must tell you that there was all the same a moment when they were going to make me head of the faculty. I only just managed to scrape out of that promotion. Tears were shed, and I had to ask my husband to intervene.

He stepped in to prevent your promotion?

Yes.

That's the first time I have heard of that kind of protectionism. It usually serves the opposite purpose.

All sorts of things happen in life. I linked my direct involvement in *perestroika* as a citizen with public work, and in particular with social work in the Soviet Culture Fund.

Tell us more about that.

There already exist in the Soviet Union today hundreds of non-governmental public funds and organizations, of which the Culture Fund was one of the first to be set up. Its emergence was the result of a general public-spirited desire to become directly involved in the democratic reforms initiated by *perestroika*, and with a desire for the spiritual renewal of life in our country. The fund began its life with the motto: preserve, develop and augment. Its tasks were: to activate interest in and attention to spiritual values and talents, to extend the circle of enthusiasts and devotees of culture, and to develop a cultural dialogue between the peoples of the Soviet Union and cultural links with the peoples of other countries. Through culture to humanize relations between people. A special concern, in my view, was to be care for the 'ecology of culture', the preservation and protection of what is known as the cultural layer in civilization which includes, as I understand it, on equal terms the works both of man and of nature. But before going any further I suggest you drink a cup of tea.

In the course of our work some little traditions had been born. One of them was to drink tea after two hours of talk, dictating and recording. While tea was being drunk the tape recorder was naturally switched off. But what Russians, and not just Russians, could drink tea in silence? Of course we conversed and chatted, and these tea-time conversations were usually of an ordinary, everyday character.

Sometimes she would talk to me about her grandchildren. I could sense that, like every grandmother, she could have said a great deal about them: I understood that she even writes down some of her half-joking half-serious observations of their behaviour. But on each occasion she restrained herself so as not to fall into the very common and, on the whole, completely forgivable sin of those who love children – talking too much about them. It is in general part of her nature to be attentive both to those around her and herself. She watches her behaviour and her appearance.

They are very different from one another, the grandchildren. They are always together, but surprisingly different. Ksenia is very emotional, kind and a great joker. She never bears a grudge. For her everybody is very good. She likes small children, music and dancing. For example, she may say something like this: 'Grandma, have you realized I am already ten – the years are flying by!' Or: 'Granny, has anything in your life made you really sad?' 'Yes,' I reply, and she says, 'I have a serious problem. I can't write the letter d properly.'

They say that Ksenia looks like me, and like Irina who also, they say, resembles me. But there is one quality that she certainly gets from Mikhail Sergeyevich, and that is her sense of humour.

Anastasia is small and quite different, well balanced and placid. She has had a strong character from the day she was born. She always knows what she wants. If she wants to eat, she will eat and there's no need to press her. If she doesn't want to eat no persuading will make her. She talks about herself in the third person. She will, for example, sit down to table and say in a reasoning voice: 'Grandma, she's fixed herself up well, hasn't she? Not bad, eh?' Or: 'Grandma, one mustn't live life too fast, true?' 'Of course,' I say. 'Anastasia, you are my little flower.' 'Grandma, I've got two legs and a flower has only one. So how can I be a little flower?' Again: 'Granny, give me a biscuit.' 'No, Anastasia, you'll get fat.' 'I'm fat as it is, so what's the difference?'

Sometimes talk about the grandchildren would be quite spontaneous – they would simply remind us of their existence themselves. Not in person – I never caught sight of either of them, though occasionally I would hear them running around and laughing.

The last time I met with Raisa Maksimovna she was only just recovering from an attack of influenza. She was wearing a long, sleeveless jacket reaching down to her knees.

Very nice, I said, taking my glass of tea.

A present, she replied, realizing at once what I was referring to. She didn't say who it was from and I didn't ask. Something in her tone of voice hinted that it was from her husband.

She reached down into the pocket of the jacket in search of her spectacles. How often in the course of those evenings had she lost her spectacles! Sometimes when she found them she would put them down in front of her on the table where they could be seen. But never once did she put them on – I never saw her in glasses. She reached into her pocket and came across a piece of paper. She laughed, because it was a note from granddaughter Ksenia to her mother (from which I gathered that the jacket was worn not only by the mother but by the daughter too, something that always happens in my home: my daughters contrive to wear not only their mother's jackets but my sweaters as well, wrapping themselves up in them as if in a shawl. The girl's note read like this:

Dear Mama,

I would like to find out from you whether we shall be
going somewhere else on my birthday apart from that
stupid polyclinic? I have in mind a café or a circus. I am
not likely to wait up for you; I shall probably go to
bed, which is why I am writing you this note.

*The ending evoked a smile — I can remember it word for word:
'I await a reply, like your nightingale, and I'm waiting for the
summer . . .' It struck me that all this — the sleeveless jacket worn
by everyone, the note in the pocket and the way it was written — bore
the stamp of the style accepted in the home and in that circle.*

So let us continue our talk about the Fund. It is headed
by Academician Dmitri Sergeyevich Likhachev, whom I had
known previously as a specialist on ancient Russian literature
and as author of *Notes on What is Russian*, reflections on Russian
culture, the peculiarities of the Russian national character,
Nature in Russia and Russian landscape painting. Dmitri
Sergeyevich told me: 'I very much want the Culture Fund to
be a fund of really great culture. We must "reach for the
heavens, for the very top".'

The Fund already has quite a few good things to its credit.
It was the father of the rebirth of charitable work in Russia
and it made its contribution to the abolition of 'blank spaces'
in our literature and history of art and to the revival and
development of various kinds of creative work.

Under the auspices of the Fund some special programmes
came into being: Local history and economy, Unique Historical
Territories, The Restoration of Forgotten Names, The Great
Silk Route, New Names, and The Preservation and Development of the Cultures of Numerically Small Peoples. A programme called Through Culture to Health and Charity has just
been set up in our country. Among organizations that have
become active are the Pushkin Society and associations of collec-

tors, bell-ringers, and restorers. A great deal of effort and enthusiasm was devoted to realizing the idea of organizing a museum for personal collections. A plan for a museum of modern art is now being put into effect. I am very pleased that the magazine of the fund called *Our Heritage*, which is printed by the Maxwell Communications Corporation, is very popular.

The Culture Fund strives to help specific useful causes in all corners of the country. In this connection I recall Mikhail Sergeyevich's visit to Sverdlovsk in April 1990. It gave me the opportunity to spend some time in places I knew as a child, in Alapayevsk, and with the backing of the Fund to support the efforts of the peoples of the Urals to develop the Alapayevsk-Sinyachka cultural complex, including the setting up of an Alapayevsk children's School of Art. That gives me much joy.

I had tremendous satisfaction from taking part in the organization of a Rorich Fund. Nikolai Rorich was a great Russian artist and thinker. As we know, he spent the last decade of his life in India but he did not break off contact with his native land. I regard it as a great blessing that Mikhail Sergeyevich and I have made the acquaintance of Svyatoslav Nikolayevich Rorich, Nikolai Rorich's son and a well-known modern artist, and his wife, Devika Rani, an Indian cinema actress and niece of Rabindranath Tagore.

I recall so well our meetings with them – our conversations that were so human and so profound: about wisdom, beauty, spirituality, goodness and 'Kanchenjunga', the sacred mountain of the 'five treasures'. And, of course, about fate.

We discussed with the Rorichs the question of setting up a Rorich Fund in Moscow and opening a Rorich cultural centre and museum. We spoke a lot about Nehru, who was at one time close to the Rorich family. Svyatoslav Nikolayevich repeated more than once that he had great faith in Mikhail Sergeyevich and that everything of his would succeed.

Rorich's speech is dotted with such old-fashioned and moving words – 'matushka moya' and 'batyushka ty moi'. His inscription on the photograph he gave us says: 'Let us always strive towards the beautiful.' It is all symbolic, like an eternal summons . . . the call of human naturalness and wisdom.

It is strange, but when I think of Rorich's work I keep recalling the fate of the Andrei Rublev Museum of ancient Russian art. I found myself in it for the first time some years ago and went through a whole range of emotions. It is impossible to underestimate the effect upon a person of the art of ancient times, whether it be articles of sculpture, of daily life, frescoes or, in the case of our Russian religious culture, ikons.

I realized that the Museum had more than enough difficulties, and I could not remain indifferent. I tried to play a part in the fate of the Museum. Unfortunately it proved to be anything but a simple task to help it out of its troubles. But I am sure it is essential to do so. Such unique museums, centres for the study of the history of Russian culture must be a matter for our common patriotic concern. We don't have many of them. Russia is not Italy.

When you travel in Italy you hear on all sides: tenth century, twelfth century, thirteenth century and so on, referring to buildings, museums and whole cities. That is why I think all our historical monuments must be better appreciated by us. We must give them more attention and care.

I think it is important that the work of such organizations as the Culture Fund should not only be based on the rebirth of morality and moral impulses coming from people, but should be capable of evoking them itself. Priceless objects and works of art and of national crafts are being handed over by the Fund's many benefactors. It all goes to replenish the displays in our museums and mobile exhibitions. But no less important in my view is the fact that people are doing it selflessly, moved by the highest motives.

What about the return of our national artistic and cultural treasures from abroad?

I want to say something about that. People, and often people not connected by birth with Russia, hand these things over, not only out of a feeling of debt to our country and not only out of generosity, but also because they have faith that they are entrusting the things into honest and good hands: the image of our country has become more attractive and more human in the years of *perestroika*. I am proud to have played some part in the return back home of our cultural treasures. It has been my good fortune to receive many such gifts, and I remember the warmth of people's hands, both old, even very old, and quite young ones, and it seems to me that that chain of warmth and concern is felt by all Soviet people at the present time, which is so difficult for us.

I would like to express gratitude to the people in America, France, Britain, Italy, Japan, Spain and other countries – to those who have emigrated from Russia, of whatever nationality they may be, as well as to those who have no formal relationship with Russia and were motivated in what they did by their own goodwill.

From the earliest time I have loved books, the theatre and painting. I value very highly inspired creative writing, and I bow down before the original, gifted mind, human dignity, courage and selflessness. I admire the beauty of the human face. As well as the beauty of the landscape, a flower and a blade of grass. It is my belief that, by protecting beauty in any of its forms, man is in the end contributing to the salvation of his own soul.

But in recent times, Raisa Maksimovna, people in Russia are talking more about 'saving one's soul' in the direct sense. There has been more active interest in the Church, in religious literature and in religious teaching and ideas. One of the reasons is probably the lack of stability in our material existence and a certain emotional strain.

Yes, probably. But it cannot be denied that the changes that have been taking place in recent years in society have, on the one hand, permitted the Church to be bolder in coming out of the shadows and ending its alienation of so many years, and, on the other hand, have made it possible for people not to conceal or to be ashamed of their beliefs, or even just their interest, even when they do not coincide with the official view. For example, that same interest in the Church. It is not a question of 'maybe', *perestroika* has definitely contributed to the rebirth of the Church and has removed certain constraints from its everyday life. Old churches and mosques are now being returned to believers. At the request of believers I have myself had occasion to take part in such handings-over, and I was glad to help a good cause. Today we hear again the ringing of church-bells on feast days, and religious sermons are even broadcast on television. Theological ideas are circulating more freely.

You remember, of course, that until 1985 even such books as the Bible and the Koran were considered to be bibliographic rarities. It was impossible to get hold of them or buy them. Today we are opening up for ourselves a rich multicoloured world inhabited by many forgotten and practically unknown thinkers and zealots of the faith and spirit. In a word, a normal dialogue with the Church is beginning in society and the State. The 'iron curtain' that existed between them until recently is coming down.

Do you remember the celebrations that marked the one thousandth anniversary of the arrival of Christianity in Russia? The Church today has joined actively in the peacemaking, charitable and patriotic work in society. This is extremely important for us. Ours is a multi-ethnic country, with people in it of many different faiths, and social accord greatly depends on all the shepherds of our multimillion flock.

I have had occasion to meet various dignitaries of the Church. I met the late Patriarch of All Russia, his Holiness Pimen, and the present Patriarch, his Holiness Aleksi II, the Roman Catholic Pope, his Holiness John-Paul II, the Supreme

Patriarch, Catholicos of all the Armenians, Vazgen I, and other spiritual leaders. And I have met ordinary believers, highly educated and deeply thinking people. His Grace Pitirim, the Metropolitan of Volokolamsk and Yurev, is a member of the Presidium of the Culture Fund. And we are now discussing together all the problems of mutual concern.

When I visit churches I invariably talk not only with the clergy but also with the ordinary believers. You see, I understand that people come to church with their pain and their anxieties, and they come in a peculiar state, bringing their pain to God. That means that we people around them failed to notice their pain and did not react to it.

Once when I visited the Svyato-Danilov monastery a woman, already old, asked me: 'Raisa Maksimovna, why did you not kneel before the ikon?' What was I to reply? So I asked her in turn: 'Do you believe in God?' 'Yes,' she replied. I said: 'Well now, that's fine. I believe a person cannot live without faith, that's what makes him a human being. But you will agree — faith can be of various kinds. Most important is: what sort of deeds does it express itself in? I know many worthy people who are atheists, I know people who do not believe in God, but believe in some kind of mysterious supreme force. Your faith does not prevent me from respecting you and your feelings and believing you. The most important thing is to be tolerant and to respect the other person's view. It is important that, in the name of some faith of our own, we don't start fighting each other or make each other suffer for it. That is my main article of faith, my ideal and my hope. So tell me now (I continued) would it really be better if, simply to humour you, to please you, I were to kneel down here?' 'No,' the woman replied, 'you mustn't be a hypocrite. That would be worse.'

Don't be a hypocrite! Those seem to me to be very important words and the key to understanding a great deal.

I am probably too interested a defender of *perestroika*, and yet among its other contributions I would mention the fact that it has returned to people a sense of their own dignity. Even that natural interest in religion, which has so increased recently, is also in the last analysis founded on that – on the revival of a sense of one's own dignity. But – don't be a hypocrite or act insincerely. To do that would be to diminish one's own dignity, would be to hurt other people's feelings and to offend them. And not only to offend them.

I am convinced that hypocrisy, the lie, is the true sister of evil, intolerance and cruelty. When I see with what ease yesterday's atheist and energetic propagandist for atheism today vows eternal loyalty to Christian dogmas, while some priest fights furiously at the barricades of political confrontation (and we have such people), I think to myself: is there in this even a single drop of faith – of any faith! – or is there only a soul-destroying lack of faith, lies and hypocrisy? Is there only that 'priceless legacy' of the past, ideological intolerance and confrontation, which it is so difficult for us to cast aside? Do you remember Evgeny Shvarts's play, *The Dragon*? The dragon, defeated by the knight Lancelot, says: my consolation is the fact that I am leaving you only ruined souls, worn-out souls, dead souls.

They say there is nothing more precious than contact with human beings. It would be difficult, even impossible, to list the names of all the people whom Mikhail Sergeyevich and I have been fortunate enough to meet in the last few years. Statesmen, politicians, public figures, scholars, artists, doctors, housewives, collective farmers, industrial workers and office workers . . . People known the world over and those not known at all. Memory preserves the moment of meeting, words, images, situations and atmosphere. They included so many talented, exceptional, brilliant and unique people! I dream of bringing them all together one day in the pages of a book.

As I accompany Mikhail Sergeyevich on his trips round

the country I often visit schools, children's homes, nurseries, hospitals, markets, shops, cultural institutions and people's homes. I do so, of course, not simply to satisfy my curiosity. My various encounters are unofficial and have a directness and degree of informality, and they provide an extra possibility for me to see and hear and understand things and if possible to help. A possibility for Mikhail Sergeyevich and me to see more.

I recall a trip in 1987 to the Murmansk region and the towns of the Soviet Polar region. I remember the majestic, severe beauty of Nature in the Far North. The very location of Murmansk was so striking – on three terraces like the three decks of an ocean liner. I remember visiting the gigantic Severonikel non-ferrous metal complex. The heroic submarine K-21 is a memorial to the courage of our fighters in the Second World War. The museum of life in the region of the northern seas. I remember very well the children and the staff at the Murmansk pre-school children's home that I was able to visit.

And, of course, I remember very well my meetings with women – in Monchegorsk, Murmansk and Severomorsk. We spoke of a lot of things: about the shortage of jobs, and the problem of finding employment for the wives of fishermen and of men serving in the armed forces. We spoke about pensions for northerners who do not want to move after they retire but want to continue living in the North. We spoke of the moral and material responsibility of parents who abandon new-born children and leave them to the mercy of fate and the care of children's homes. It is a problem in Murmansk and in other ports. We spoke of the quality of the food provided in the children's homes and the provision of the homes and boarding schools with transport. We also spoke of everyday problems and about ecology in Monchegorsk. We spoke of the part that the women of Murmansk could play in the work of the Culture Fund and in the development of cultural links with people living in the neighbouring Scandinavian countries. And I am pleased that in dealing with certain 'women's' problems in the area I have taken a part and made a contribution, however small.

Along with the Chairman of the Murmansk region council for women, Margarita Mikhailovna Molodtsova, I prepared a note concerning the most pressing social problems and sent it to the Central Committee of the CPSU and the Council of Ministers of the USSR. Some of the proposals made by the women's councils in Murmansk and ideas put forward by the Party and government organizations in Murmansk – concerning problems of women, children and elderly people living in the North – were sent to the Presidium of the Supreme Soviet of the USSR, to the Soviet Women's Committee and to the Children's Fund. There were general resolutions summing up the results of Mikhail Sergeyevich's trip, touching on a whole series of problems, and our proposals were included in them.

I am not, of course, in a position to help with everything I come across or about which people write to me with requests. And although my heart aches and although, believe me, I would like to help everyone, one has to face the reality of life and recognize that no one is almighty. Most difficult of all are questions of housing, serious illness, the fate of invalids and of single elderly persons.

In the last few years I have heard quite a few kind words addressed to me. I have also acquired my own supporters, allies and friends, both here at home and abroad – in the United States there is even a society of friends of Raisa Gorbachev. I thank them all, my friends far and near, for their support, their good feelings and kind words. The pictures that have been presented to me, the books, poems, songs and drawings – what could be more precious than such sincere gestures? And the messages – simple, sincere and trusting: 'With respect for you and gratitude for your courage and distinguished representation of the women of our country to the whole world. K. Tishchenko, Krivoi Rog.'

I am going through quite recent mail: 'Dear Raisa Maksimovna! I congratulate you on the holiday of the 8th of March. I wish you Siberian health, Caucasian long life, the peace and love of your family, and, of course, patience. I understand how difficult it is to be the wife of the President, but everything will be all right. I pray for you and await your call. There is a great deal that must be said. Respectfully, Raisa Alekseyevna Mukharamova. Ashkhabad.' Here's one from Ivano-Frankovsk, from the family of a man who fought in the Great Patriotic War. Congratulations on the 8th of March. 'On this beautiful day we present you with a million snowdrops . . .'

This letter is from the USA – from Gloria Hatten Sapp, who lives in the state of Georgia.

Dear Mrs Gorbachev

I sat in my home watching and listening to your first speech delivered to the students at Wellesley College and to the viewing public of the United States of America.

I do not know how the citizens of the Soviet Union hold you in their opinions; I hope it is with the tremendous respect you deserve.

Your words were inspiring, your poise was graceful, and your sentiments were shared by thousands. Your presence helped bridge the gap between our nations; a gap that is growing smaller and smaller at a quickening pace.

I wish you, your husband and your country triumph over the obstacles you face. I am thankful for all that you are and all that you are accomplishing for our world.

Most respectfully, Gloria Hatten Sapp.

Now here is another letter which I will read in its entirety.

Dear Raisa Maksimovna!

I don't know whether this letter will reach you or whether I ought to be writing it. But, believe me, I very much want to say some kind words to you. Frankly speaking, when Mikhail Sergeyevich began to make trips round our country and you joined in those trips, which were anything but tourist excursions but real working occasions, I was rather annoyed. But some time later after your first trips I realized that they were actually work for you and not pleasure trips. And it was anything but easy work. It is a great social work and a moral obligation. Whatever your mood or state of health you have to smile at the journalists and the people around you. You have to understand what people are talking about and talk with people and reply to their questions, not with superficial answers, for the sake of answering, but much more seriously, knowing what their problems are and replying to all their questions. Then there is your ability to dress modestly but at the same time with taste and in accordance with the fashion. And you have the ability as a woman to dispose people towards you. In my view, to be the wife of the General Secretary is very difficult, when you are seen not just as a woman in general but as the wife of Mikhail Sergeyevich. It really is a very difficult job! I am writing this letter after watching the *Vremya* programme on the television, which showed you on your visit to Yugoslavia. And, my word of honour, I felt really proud of you, Mikhail Sergeyevich, Soviet people and my country. Maybe my letter is rather confused and not all of it will be clear to you. I simply want you to understand my good will and best feelings towards you. Larisa Gutsal. 28 years of age.'

Here is another letter, from Italy:

Raisa – that's the way they address you, without any
titles or adjectives. We love you for the way you appear
side by side with Signor President – modestly, quietly
and intelligently but at the same time lovingly. Confident,
calm and serene. You move, sowing the seeds of spring
which are already producing shoots of the flowers of
freedom and of joy. May your strength not betray you
further on this path. Thank you.

Sister Anna Lonero. Naples.

Well, that's not prose but poetry.

I am deeply grateful to the five million readers of the British
magazine *Woman's Own* who chose me as 'woman of the year'
and awarded me in 1987 a prize for my international work. I
am grateful to the international fund 'Together for Peace' and
its chairman Signora Fanfani for awarding me the prize
'Women for Peace'. I was touched to the depths of my heart
to learn that Mr Rivello in Italy, the Modzelewsky family in
the USA, the Rejin family in Brazil and the Dimov family in
Bulgaria had called their children by my name. A Polish firm,
Vitroflora, and its owners, husband and wife Anna and Karol
Pavlak, have developed a beautiful and amazing new sort of
flower and called it 'Raisa'. A firm in the Federal German
Republic, Ogilvy and Meiser Fokas, has given my name to a
new kind of rose they have developed.

Believe me, I by no means seek such marks of attention.
I do not thirst for such general adoration. But that's the way
the human heart is made: it makes no mistake in detecting
other people's goodwill and their attitude towards you. That
is its best source of nourishment. It reacts to goodness with
goodness immediately.

I remember Sicily, Messina, the town of Linz in the outskirts of Bonn, Minneapolis . . . I shall preserve in my heart
forever the gratitude I feel towards all those people who came

forward in those memorable days to shake my hand and through me to express their confidence and gratitude to my country, my people and my husband.

And yet it is not by chance that we Russians have a saying that 'you can't be nice to the whole world'. And it sometimes happens that the 'world' turns out to be kinder to you than 'home'.

It happens . . . In recent years I have, of course, heard other things said: that I have 'pretensions to play some special role', that I am 'meddling in things that don't concern me', that I am 'the Kremlin's secret weapon', that I am the 'tsaritsa', Josephine, and so on.

I believe, Georgi Vladimirovich, that it is not so much my individuality and not just the variety of human thought, attitudes and assessments that determine the contradictory nature of people's judgements. In my view, on the whole it is other circumstances that are important. Possibly it is primarily the fact of my appearing openly in public.

The essence of the matter is that the concept of 'wife of the leader of the Party and the country' became with us very abstract. It really said nothing. It is a matter here not only of the wife of the leader of the State. It seems to me to go deeper. It is a question of the attitude toward women as a whole, and especially to woman as a wife and woman as a mother, and of their position in our society. I have already discussed with you the fact that, having done quite a lot for women and children, the country was still not able to create the necessary conditions for realizing Soviet woman's equality in practice and for the assertion of her human dignity with full rights. Moreover there has been a re-evaluation downwards in the social awareness and in public opinion of the role of the family. At the same time there has been a depreciation of the role of the woman as mother and the woman as wife and – don't rush to conclusions – of the man as father. Oh yes, the reduction in the role of the woman inevitably reduced the importance of the man in

the family. The two are related. A typical detail: I remember
that, when I was still a child, the family observed all holidays
and celebrations, both public and family, together. Father and
mother would go out always together, whether it was to visit
friends or to the club for official celebrations and occasions.

The following situation, for example, was not exceptional
but quite natural. My father would have a formal meeting at
his work. Among other leading workers he would be presented
with an honorary certificate or a prize, while my mother would
be there in the audience along with other wives of my father's
colleagues. After the formalities were over, along with my
classmates, I would appear on the wooden stage where my
father had just been honoured. A concert would follow. We
would sing and dance for the workers and construct a pyramid
of gymnasts . . . And I knew that the most appreciative, the
most intent and most 'suffering' of my audience were my father
and mother sitting side by side somewhere in the front rows.
The whole family would go for a picnic or a spring outing,
and transport was even allotted for it so that entire families
could take part in some event, always with the children.

Nowadays, you know, colleagues at work celebrate people's
birthdays without their wives or husbands. For national celebrations wives and husbands are not invited. Even a group
visit to the theatre is organized on the basis of the collective
at work. 'Tickets according to the number of members of the
trade union!' – who has not heard those words? It has also
become fashionable to go on leave or on holiday as a single
person. It is a problem to obtain a holiday package for a whole
family. Do we have many boarding-houses or rest homes where
families can stay? Practically none. We didn't think about it.
We reckoned we were building something better than the
family.

Incidentally, it is only in our country and in a few countries
that used to be close to us that official receptions and dinners
take place without wives or spouses. In my view there could

be fewer such receptions, but it would be much better, more appropriate if wives were invited as is the practice in the rest of the world. And what happens when a highly placed official, speaking in the Supreme Soviet of the Russian Federation and watched by the 300 million television audience, insults his colleague, a woman? Somebody's wife and mother. When he was asked to apologize he gave the impression of not knowing what he was to apologize for.

In both the material and the moral sense we have cheapened the value of the work that women do in the home and the family. It has now become not only bad form but practically 'improper' to be proud of a wife who is a housewife or to describe your partner in life in such a way. Here again and again I think of my mother. Yes, she was also a housewife. But, you know, she brought up three children, and what could be more to the benefit of the State than the work involved in that? She gave all her children, I repeat, an excellent education, all on our father's very modest income. In order to manage in such conditions there had to be devotion to work and even, forgive me, real talent. Her hands, on which so much depended, were not only hard-working, they were also talented. She sewed, altered, turned, cooked, washed, cleaned, cultivated the garden, looked after the cow and the chicken, treated the children when they were sick and watched every kopek, and that's also a talent and a real one! It requires a lot of character and energy to run a house and a family. What a pity that we don't know how to appreciate it!

Is it only the housewife who it is not fashionable to praise today? I believe that the situation of women and the family in the State is our common concern. Quite recently I read somewhere that, if the women are happy, the whole of society will be happy. Everybody cannot, of course, be happy at once, but it's a very interesting thought just the same.

I am interested in something else I have observed. Following the devaluation of the role of the father, mother and wife, perhaps simultaneously, some irreversible processes have begun to take place in connection with the very concept of the home.

What do you have in mind?

I will explain. The attachment to the family home, which used to be so typical of everybody, began to decline and lose its strength. 'State-owned' housing came to be preferred to one's own home, lived in for generations. I am not speaking only of the parental homes around the country that have been abandoned and deserted. By continually moving ourselves from one apartment to another, from a communal apartment to a small separate apartment and then one day from the small one to a better one, and obtaining each one by fighting for it and overcoming all the obstacles, we become willy-nilly enthusiastic practitioners of the 'exchange'. Of the process itself. We don't have time to become attached to anything, or make a place comfortable and homely before it's time to 'spread out' or to move on. Perhaps that is why we do not take care of or value especially the state-owned apartments or houses and don't worry about them as we would worry about our own. We are always on the move, always lodgers.

At the time of Mikhail Sergeyevich's meeting with George Bush in Malta I spent some time with a young Maltese family. They were newly married, charming and welcoming and did not yet have children. But the flat already had a children's room and they were already equipping it quietly. The apartment was three-roomed which they had purchased on a mortgage with their parents' help. They had immediately bought an apartment that allowed for the family to expand and which would last them a long time, perhaps for more than one generation. That is how you lay the foundations of a family home. It is built as the swallows build their nests. Russia is not Malta, of course. The scale is different, including the extent of the shortages of accommodation. We can't for the time being, even for money, provide every young family with the possibility of having an apartment like that, spacious, permanent and with provision for the future. But something could be done even now! If a person lives in the house in which his mother and father lived he has a different attitude to its walls, and not just its walls. He has a more stable attitude to life and has deeper roots in it. After all, a house is not just its walls, it is something else that cannot be put into words, something mysterious.

Once again I remember my mother. I have already told you that we also had no permanent home: we trooped endlessly in the wake of my father the railway worker, endlessly changing our abode. But wherever we went, wherever we moved to, my mother stubbornly carted along with us an old sideboard, as if it were something very precious and living. Wherever we found ourselves that sideboard would be put in place, and we already had a home. There was already something of our own. Whatever you thought of it, it was our 'nest'. It brought warmth and security to us. And we never parted with that sideboard. It provided a link between Mother and all of us with those who in the past had composed our home.

It is difficult to believe what I am about to tell you, but it so fits in with your story. I had the good fortune to be with you on a visit to Turgenev's house in Bougival. And do you know what struck me most of all? I remember that my mother had a cupboard made, if I am not mistaken, of the dark wood of the plane tree. There was not a single nail in the whole cupboard or its shelves. It had been handed down to her by her mother who had also received it from her mother. It was, as I now realize, the most valuable object in our home. It was, of course, already falling to pieces, but the wood was light, mature and sweet smelling. I liked to stick my nose into the cupboard, not just in search of something tasty but simply to smell the air inside it — spicy, delicious and mysterious. But my mother died and I stupidly tried to make a sleigh out of the upper shelves. I tried sawing, but the wood would not saw; I knocked in some nails and the wood split. In short I ruined the cupboard. Later the house was sold, we children were sent off to children's homes or boarding schools, and the things in the house were also sold or lost. The cupboard also vanished, like everything else. An old linen tablecloth remained and is with us still as a memento of my mother. And, with the passing of the years, I began more often and more painfully to recall that cupboard, perhaps because I felt guilty about it. For me it really was 'deeply respected' as in Chekhov's The Cherry Orchard. *You can be nostalgic about things as well. So thirty years later I visited Turgenev's house, now a museum, and what do you think was the first thing to catch my eye?*

I can guess.

Yes, it was an antique cupboard in dark wood and, as it seemed to me, exactly the same as the one my late mother had in my parents' house. I was really shaken and spent practically the whole of the visit standing by it. I wanted to open the door, put my head into its spicy depths and sniff!

That's what you should have done. As I recall, the people in charge of the museum were hospitable and simple people. But in general I understand you very well. The feeling of home is something one must not lose, that is dangerous. Every one of us must try to revive it. It is also the way to finding a sound foundation, putting down roots and gaining stability in every person's heart and in society. My house is not just my castle: it is also my world, my galaxy. That's what I think. Moreover we must from childhood stop driving out of children the desire to work by giving them formal handicraft lessons 'work training', which most often teach them only how to wriggle out of any obligation to perform mandatory work, and give them the freedom to work themselves, wherever they want and where it is not harmful to their health. Best of all — in their own homes, orchard or market garden.

Nowadays many of them simply dream of that — to have their own home and garden. Grown-ups as well as children, including my own. It seems that this is true on a global scale. In America the boom in private home building and gardening was associated with the fact that people born in the post-war years are now entering their active working life. It is the generation of the 'baby-boom'. I think it also has direct relation to us. I personally believe and have great hopes in my generation — and I would like it not to be the generation of those who have 'nothing to lose', but of socialist property owners.

I would do everything possible to encourage such a tendency. I would encourage everything that binds a person to his home, to his native soil, to a given order of things and gives him greater stability in society and the opportunity honestly to increase his wealth. It is time, already time, to stop shouting and howling and whipping up intolerance, hatred and bad feeling and to start doing something positive — in the home. I also believe in hard-working and businesslike — my mother would have said 'busy' — people, and I am impatient to see more of them on the path of *perestroika*.

To finish with the subject of the home: this spring the President had planned to fly down for his mother's eightieth birthday. He wanted to go on his own — that I know for sure. But as it happened the miners wouldn't let him go. In his place went people who were to some extent able to replace him and give his mother pleasure comparable with the arrival of her son.

Two personal representatives of the President flew down for the occasion: two little emissaries with bows in their hair — Ksenia and Anastasia.

His mother was happy, though at the same time sad — a state familiar to all our mothers, irrespective of whether they are waiting patiently on the family threshold for a president, a prime minister or a general labourer. The fact that he is a son says everything.

We started our conversation, Raisa Maksimovna, about the position in society of the wife of the country's leader.

Actually, throughout the civilized world the position, rights and duties of the wife of the head of state are more or less clearly laid down, either in some written regulations or according to certain traditions. For example, I was told that in the White House, to assist the President's wife to carry out her official functions at the proper level, there is the necessary staff. There is a person in charge of the office and the President's wife even has her own 'territory' and her own 'office' in a wing of the White House. Madame Mitterrand, wife of the President of France, who devotes a great deal of effort to the organization France Liberté which she founded, acquainted me on one visit to France with the work of her own secretariat which, as a matter of tradition, helps the President's wife in her social and charitable work. Frau Kohl is very active and engaged in very varied social work and guardianship, and she also told me about the special office set up to give her the necessary assistance.

It turned out, Georgi Vladimirovich, that I had at my disposal only one tradition, which took shape in Stalin's day – the absence of any right to a public, official existence. It even strikes me occasionally that a certain section of our society regarded my public appearance with excessive partiality, as if it were the 'big event' of *perestroika*.

Yes, my appearance in public alongside Mikhail Sergeyevich required of me as wife of the head of state that I should carry out certain official duties: taking part in meetings and certain government and social functions including some involving protocol. I did not, of course, have any special diplomatic knowledge and certainly no experience of 'high society'. I learnt as I went along, using my own everyday logic and intuition.

I really acquired a great deal through intuition, and through a natural tendency to use my common sense. I learnt for the first time in detail that there are strict rules governing diplomatic ceremonies and protocol in international affairs. There are general rules that are accepted in all international practice,

and there are special, national rules and requirements of protocol connected with the different traditions of particular peoples
and states. I learnt – no longer by hearsay but from 'primary
sources' – that even such occasions as a 'lunch', 'tea' or 'four-
chette' have their own 'individual' elements of diplomatic etiquette. For example, the 'dinner' is the most important kind
of reception, which has to take place in the evening after seven
o'clock or later, although it is called a dinner. It requires a
strict and well-defined order of 'seating' at table and, as a rule,
formal or evening attire.

In some countries women are expected to appear in long
evening dresses at official lunches. In our everyday life a long
dress is something not very necessary, and in my opinion not
necessary at all. Very elegant, of course, but it is a requirement
that is rather wasteful to observe – do you often attend such
'dinners'? Again, it is a very small matter, but in 1985 a new
rule was adopted in the diplomatic protocol of our country: at
official receptions and dinners in our country now it is required
only that the men should wear dark suits and the women
elegant dresses of ordinary length.

We can reckon that our protocol is the most economical in the world!

Not the most economical, Georgi Vladimirovich, but the
most democratic.

Every form of representation requires attention to the peculiarities in the everyday life, the traditions and customs of the
people and the country. Attention to both big and small matters. I remember with gratitude, for example, with what
understanding Mrs Bush and the staff of Wellesley College
treated my request that, when I attended the commencement,
I should not have to put on the academic gown and headgear,
because it was not the practice in our country. It would have
embarrassed me and I would have felt very awkward in it.

As the place for Mikhail Sergeyevich to make his speech on
our last visit to Britain the British government proposed the

Guildhall, an extremely prestigious building in London which is the centre of the financial world, the City. It is an honour only very rarely extended to foreign guests and a mark of special respect. But in accordance with ancient tradition a ceremony in the Guildhall presupposes certain obligatory forms of dress: a woman must wear a hat and gloves and a man tails, a morning coat or military uniform.

An exception was made in our case. Mrs Thatcher respected our wishes and, contrary to tradition, decided that she, too, would not wear a hat or gloves. During the same visit Mikhail Sergeyevich and I went to Windsor and met the Queen. In England an audience of the Queen is the highest mark of diplomatic esteem. I had already learnt that Queen Elizabeth's favourite colour was blue – 'royal blue' – and usually appears somewhere in her attire. I also gathered that members of the royal family and guests of the Queen tried not to use that colour when they were in her presence. I also tried to maintain the tradition.

In the course of official visits by heads of state it is the tradition for the hosts to propose a separate and additional programme for the visitor's wife, apart from the official visit itself. Such a programme is usually agreed beforehand through the foreign ministry. The hosts take account of the interests and wishes of the guests, but above all, of course, the guest also has to bear in mind the possibilities and the suggestions made by the hosts. I have sometimes heard people who were along with me, my own compatriots, say about programmes arranged for me: 'Raisa Maksimovna, do you really find that interesting? Can you really not think of something different?' You can think of something, but you certainly can't carry it out always. But quietly, discreetly, I also manage to slip away from a strictly arranged programme. In Finland in 1990 I got away 'incognito' to look at the 'church in the cliff' and to wander round the streets of Helsinki. In San Francisco, apart from the agreed programme, I undertook a sortie to the coastal district of the city, spent some time in Chinatown, in a family grocer's shop and on the platform of a sightseeing tram and talked to the conductor. She was so moved that she offered me the favour of making use of the services of her friend, a hair-dresser who would, she said, give me a beautiful American hair-do.

I particularly remember the grocer's shop. The right to choose which shop rested with the head of security on the American side. Your 'escape' was, of course, entirely his responsibility. He was not very talkative — mostly he just smiled into his moustache — but very imposing and greying at the temples. The spitting image of Faulkner in his prime. But when we entered the store with you I was simply dazzled — bottles, bottles and more bottles to suit any taste! Good old 'Faulkner' — he knew where to go!

Yes, it certainly was a well-stocked wine department. The other sections were also very good. In France, in a little café called the Rosarie in Bougival, I drank coffee with some French women and had a purely women's conversation with them — not in the least diplomatic.

Some misunderstandings as regards the rules of diplomatic procedure must have been, in my view, the basis for the rumours spread in the American press about 'friction' between Nancy Reagan and myself. I did not take, and I still don't take, those statements seriously. Nancy Reagan and I were lucky because we were witnesses of, and in some respects participants in, the greatest and most important historic meet-ings between the leaders of our two countries. All our feelings, worries and anxieties were just a drop in the ocean of the hope born of these meetings and felt by people throughout the world: the hope of peace and a future for the whole of mankind.

I remember the first meeting in Geneva in November 1985. They got to know each other, studied each other, 'adjusted' to each other and had debates and discussions. The birth of understanding was difficult, as was the drafting of the official documents. I remember the mansion, the Maison de Saussure, where Ronald and Nancy Reagan gave an official dinner in honour of Mikhail Sergeyevich and myself. We were still in the mansion at two o'clock in the morning. That morning we were due to fly out of Geneva but they just couldn't arrive at a final draft of the joint statement. Every sentence, every word and every letter was fought over. All the same, Geneva gave birth to what was most important – a recognition that a nuclear war cannot be won and must not be fought.

After Geneva a revival began to take place in scientific, cultural and economic contacts between our countries that had previously been at a standstill or had not existed at all. Then came October 1986 and the meeting in Reykjavik, Iceland. How much has already been written about that Soviet–American summit meeting and its dramatic events! Yes, we all went through that, but we remember and understand its importance too – for without Reykjavik there would not have been Washington in 1987 or Moscow in 1988. There would not have taken place the meetings that turned out to be more constructive and more productive of results than the meeting in Geneva. There would have been no Treaty on the destruction of intermediate- and short-range missiles. And there would not have been that rare human mutual understanding and accord of the Soviet and American peoples that became apparent clearly and strikingly in December 1987 in Washington, in 1988 in New York, in Washington, Minnesota, and in San Francisco in 1990. There was accord in the name of peace and friendship.

In Geneva Nancy Reagan and I took part in the laying of a stone for the building of a museum of the International Red Cross. Today the museum is already open. I would like it and all the work done by the International Red Cross and Red Crescent to symbolize for ever collaboration between all states and peoples in the cause of mutual understanding and trust and in the name of goodness and charity.

Out of the mass of impressions that remain in my mind after Mikhail Sergeyevich's trips to various countries the most important is that of thousands of open, friendly human faces. I remember Delhi, New York, Minnesota, Prague, Crakow, Stettin, Berlin, Dortmund, Stuttgart, Shanghai, Madrid, Barcelona, Rome, Messina, Milan, Nagasaki . . . The crowded streets and squares of the cities. Sympathy and friendship on people's faces. Hope and faith in people's hearts and eyes: the belief that the world can survive without the use of force, that the world can be without war.

Italy, the country of Dante and Petrarch. The source of European civilization. And the cathedral square in Milan with the amazingly beautiful decorated marble façade of the cathedral itself. Monuments everywhere to a great culture. And the equally amazing and unforgettable outpouring of emotion by the many, many thousands of people gathered there as the people of Milan welcomed Mikhail Sergeyevich and the delegation. 'Gorby, Gorby, Gorby!' they were shouting in the square. Eduard Amvrosievich Shevardnadze and I were walking together. We had been left behind by Mikhail Sergeyevich and had to make our way through the dense crowd of people. I looked at him and saw that there were tears in his eyes, as there were in mine. He said to me then: 'For the sake of this too it was worth while to begin *perestroika.*'

I keep on repeating to myself, and not only to myself, one and the same question: ought Eduard Amvrosievich, a friend of Mikhail Sergeyevich and one who shares his views, to have brought it to an end in such a way? I have preserved the letter that Shevardnadze wrote on his sixtieth birthday, that was such a special day for him and for us, his friends.

Dear Mikhail Sergeyevich and Raisa Maksimovna,
    This day in my life, a major award from my country, and the kind words you addressed to me on the occasion of my sixtieth birthday give me the moral right to express

to you my heartfelt thanks. All the same, I would like in this written reaction to your congratulations and good wishes to go beyond the limits of what is for me an important day.

It would be more correct, in my view, to speak of the importance of the whole period in the life of the Party and country of which my life and my work in the post I was appointed to is only a small particle.

At a reception in the Soviet embassy in Madrid recently an elderly Spaniard, who was far from sharing our ideas but who had suffered agonizingly the tragedy of the 1930s and the long night of Franco's rule, said: 'At last people have appeared in world affairs with high ideals and pure intentions, knights without fear or blame, like Don Quixote to our Spanish way of thinking. At last a great human ambition has received a wonderful human embodiment.'

It was you he had in mind.

You will remember what great personal anxiety and doubt attended my new appointment. I am still not free of them. At every step, every day and every hour I experience a colossal 'resistance of the material'. But, both just over two years ago and today, I found and I find now the strength in myself to overcome that resistance. The source of that strength is certainly not to be found in the fact that I succeeded in fully mastering the complicated art of the new type of diplomacy, the diplomacy of the period of new political thinking: we have a long way to go for that. I see the sources of my strength in something else.

I see it in your support which I felt and still feel in the hours and days of the most trying ordeals. I see it in the policy that you have devised, of which the honesty, universal appeal and scientific underpinning make it irresistible for millions of people. I see it in the positions

taken up by the Party, society and the country – the
positions that the world rightly identifies with you.

For a large part of my life I too served the Party's cause
as well as I could. I have never concealed and do not
conceal now that I had my doubts, some uneasy thoughts,
and occasionally inner disagreement, but they were
always kept down by my faith that the decisive and
critical hour would strike for our Motherland. Now that it
has struck I feel for the first time that my life is in
complete accord with the life of the Party and the
people.

It is a great source of happiness, and I am indebted to
you for it. I know of no better award to myself. And I
know no better response to it than to be always near you
in the front ranks of *perestroika*.

That Spaniard was right about everything, except one:
we are not dealing with windmills. But all the obstacles in
our path can be brought down and we will revive the
country for a life of happiness in a rejoicing humanity.
I believed this and I still believe.

Yours ever,
E. Shevardnadze

Even now I am very moved by what is said in that letter . . .

People have often asked me and still ask me: is it an easy
life to be wife of the President and General Secretary of the
Party? I always reply that it is easier than actually being the
President and General Secretary. I do not take any state or
political decisions, do not take part in their preparation, and
bear no responsibility for them. My work is purely social.
Everything I do falls within that framework. So much for that.
But the President and General Secretary is my husband. His
life is also my life. His worries are also my worries. Can the
anxiety for our country, which makes itself felt today in the
heart of every thinking Soviet citizen, pass my heart by?

When I attend the Congress of People's Deputies of the USSR in the Kremlin Palace of Congresses I sit among the people invited in the gallery and a lot of people come up to me – Deputies, guests and correspondents. They put questions to me, ask my opinion, and thank me for being present along with them in the hall. But some actually say: 'Why do you do it? You just don't spare yourself, Raisa Maksimovna. Why do you upset your nerves and your mind, why?' Once when I was talking with our talented and popular singer Alla Borisovna Pugacheva I heard her say: 'I cannot sing to a theme, Raisa Maksimovna – it has to be from my heart.' I understand her. I can't live to a 'theme'. I can't live without putting my whole heart into everything I live by, into everything I do, in which I am involved and for which I am responsible.

I remember another episode that took place, it is true, not in Moscow but in Paris. Mikhail Sergeyevich and I have visited the city several times and it so happened that on two occasions I had as my French guide and protector a very pretty girl called Isabel. On the last occasion, just before we were leaving, I had a curious conversation with her.

'Madame,' she said, 'in the course of my duties I see a lot of important people. I am worried about you. You are like me. It's going to be very difficult for you.'

'Why, Isabel?'

'You are too open, you worry about everything.'

'So what can I do?' I asked.

The girl shrugged her shoulders.

But I remember another episode involving that girl.

Which was that?

You praised her for the elegance of her style of dress in the presence of other people, and she blushed with pleasure. Next day she appeared in even more stylish attire that in no way resembled a police uniform, even in Paris.

Well, that's all very true. A woman is always a woman.

Our country is going through a difficult time, a very diffi-cult time at present. The choice has been made. It remains firm and constant. Our society has set out on the path of renewal and of demolishing totalitarianism and the obsolete command system of administering the country. There is no way back. Only forwards, only along the path of democratiz-ation, national revival and the realization of further political, legal and economic reforms. But there are so many difficulties that have arisen and are still arising on that path!

The endless 'black holes' that have been exposed in the economy, ecology, culture, medicine, social security and the defence of people's rights in the *perestroika* period were pre-viously camouflaged and concealed. It turned out that we, society as a whole, did not know the real, factual state of affairs in all areas of our life. *Perestroika* has had to cope with Chernobyl, the earthquake in Armenia and the events in Nagorno Karabakh, Sumgait, Osh, Southern Ossetia, Baku and Lithuania . . . We have had thousands of refugees within our own country!

The period of *perestroika* is by no means easy or simple. All those dramatic events were a testing of the spirit, the mind and the will. They involve incurable heartache and sleepless nights. The telephone rings out like a gunshot destroying the peace of the night. Nowadays telephones frighten me. They bring shouts of despair, entreaties, suffering and, sometimes, someone's death.

I remember all those terrible nights – from the time of Chernobyl to the crisis in the Persian Gulf, when at two-twenty in the morning Mikhail Sergeyevich was informed that the operation was due to start in an hour's time and Iraq was to be bombed. There was the night of the 19th to the 20th of January 1990 – the night of the events in Baku. I recall that next day I could scarcely recognize Mikhail Sergeyevich – he had gone grey and his face was grey too: he seemed to have suffered a nervous shock, to have gone through a mental crisis.

And, you know, I was not alone in noticing the trauma that he went through. I have just come across an amazing letter, written on the 24th of January. It was delivered to the editorial office of the newspaper *Pravda* but it was addressed to Mikhail Sergeyevich. It is from the town of Panevezhis and written by Yu. I. Vasilyauskas.

Mikhail Sergeyevich! If there is a God or some other supreme force may you be granted the best possible health and fortitude, especially now. I am simply afraid that you will give in and get away from all those people who are now, openly or covertly, hissing and gloating because of the fighting in the Caucasus. Why did I decide to write to you? Simply because for the first time I saw such sadness in your eyes when you spoke on the television about the events in Azerbaidzhan. I will not enter into any long discussion here, only to say: I understand perfectly well the feelings of a person who gives everything he can to people and tries to do his best and yet is often met with, it seems to me, only black ingratitude. I understand very well that in that case a man simply feels like saying: live as you please! That is a purely human reaction and it is to be understood. But, my dear Mikhail Sergeyevich, you often say in your speeches that without this or that *perestroika* will fail . . . I am your most convinced supporter as a matter of principle, although like everyone I can have my own opinion. You know how to persuade people, that's a fact. But on one thing no one, even you, will persuade me that I am wrong: that if you now, because you are offended or for some other reason, decide to quit that that would be an end to *perestroika*. That is a thousand per cent right! You must not do it for any reason, not in any circumstances, you must not. It must not be permitted. If you quit now it will be the end of everything.

Perestroika has already become a rather trite word, and therefore I say that your departure in the present conditions would signify the end of the hopes of all those who believe that after all there is light at the end of the tunnel . . . People are far from being angels, but what can one do? You have chosen your path, and however hard it may be you must carry on to the end. You must not quit! Not for anything! Therefore, even if you are put under pressure and accused of making mistakes, hold on, don't get depressed. I beg it of you. I simply do not understand how people, if they only exert a little thought, can fail to approve what you are doing and in any case do not understand one thing that seems to me to be elementary. It is something that ought to be clear even to an amoeba: that you are working exclusively for the benefit of people in our country and the world. That is your supreme objective, and it will not be seen only by a person who is blind or who does not wish to see. I don't take part in any demonstrations, neither for nor against, and I don't belong to any party. But I always support, without any qualifications, your policy, your aims and your ideas. Without you there would be nothing. I am not a stupid sheep or bootlicker and I don't need anything. I appreciate that you have the right to drop everything. But for God's sake, Mikhail Sergeyevich, not at this moment, whatever anybody says. God grant that I am mistaken and that my fears are unfounded, for God's sake. But one can draw such a conclusion from scraps of information and various rumours. Moreover, at the second Congress you said several times: let anyone who wishes take my place, I'm not hanging on to it. God grant that you said that in the heat of the moment.

Everything you have done so far, everything you have
succeeded in doing, is not yet irreversible. Everything
could still go into reverse if you quit. Don't do it, I
entreat you! I am convinced that I am not alone in my
opinion. There are millions of people who think as I do.
And not in the West, but here throughout our country.

Remember that all our hopes are centred in you. If my
fears are unfounded, then thank the Lord for that! Forgive
me for mentioning the name of the divinity so often – I
am not a believer. But if I were I would pray to God
that my letter should not have been written in vain. And
forgive me for the confused nature of this letter. Perhaps
in this case it will convince you of its sincerity. I remain
your most convinced supporter. I wish you and those
near to you all the very best. And again I wish you to
persevere and to persevere to the end. Forgive me for
bothering you.

It is a very emotional but also reasonable and sensible letter.
I trust its author more than those people who keep saying,
with obviously provocative intent in mind and with enviable
persistence at this difficult time, that you can't carry out a
revolution in white gloves. I have heard Mikhail Sergeyevich
say more than once that the goals that we have set ourselves
do not permit us to be indiscriminate in our choice of means
to achieve them.

*At a meeting of Secretaries of local Party organizations at the 28th
Congress of the CPSU one of the women there, an Azerbaidzhanian,
threw the charge at the General Secretary that amounted to accusing
him of being the butcher of the people of Azerbaidzhan. He rose slowly
from his seat and said, not immediately: 'You know, it is impossible
to live with such an accusation.' There was an uproar in the hall,
and the woman apologized . . .*

Today, when the economic situation has become so difficult

as well as the living conditions of the people as a whole, decisions have to be taken that are extremely hard. But they must be taken. It is obvious that they can no longer be put off. They have been put off too long . . .

But, you know, today it is not only problems of a material character that are putting pressure on us. *Perestroika*, democratization and *glasnost* have made intellectual life in our society and life as a whole freer and more open. The social consciousness has been freed from many obsolete stereotypes and dogmas, the acceptance of the diversity of opinions has made it possible to take a new look at our history, the present day and the world around us. It has become apparent that there is a great variety of views and interests in different sections of society. But here too we have come up against very serious, and perhaps the most serious, problems.

Nationalism and extremism have come to the surface. They are spreading today like a cancerous growth in the fabric of people's national self-awareness. It so happens that I have both Russian and Ukrainian roots. My father, as you know, came from the Chernigov area, while I was born in the Altai region, lived in Siberia, the Urals, Bashkiria and the Caucasus with its very mixed national composition. For almost twenty years I have been living in Moscow. I have a good idea of what is meant by mutual relationships and links and mutual help between people of various nationalities. I am profoundly convinced that that is the invisible medium in which alone it is possible for each separate human life and our human civilization itself to survive. That is what made it possible for us to hold out, to endure or, as my mother would have said, to 'make it through' the bitterest years and days experienced by our Motherland. And I find it extremely alarming when I see holes appearing in that priceless medium for human morality.

I was first struck by this with terrible force in Armenia, at the time of the tragic earthquake. If you recall, Mikhail Sergeyevich then broke off his official visit to the United States and, after a brief stop-over in Moscow, arrived at the very centre of that frightful disaster. We visited Leninakan, Spitak and Kirovokan. I shall never forget those days! Nor shall I forget the people's faces. There was so much sorrow in their piercing looks.

I saw men driven frantic by the weight of their loss and I saw women sobbing over tiny graves and did what I could to console them. I saw crippled children in the hospitals. Like any adult person I looked into their eyes not only with fear but also with a feeling of guilt. Yes, it had been a natural disaster. Man had practically nothing to do with it. But I know that, whatever happened, whatever befell people, a person can never feel himself aloof from human suffering and tragedy. For that reason moments of the greatest tragedy, such as happen in the course of human life, become also moments of uplift for the human spirit and human virtue. Incidentally, those days were full of that dramatic combination – of disaster and the heartfelt, nationwide, even worldwide reaction to it.

The country remembered that it was one country and that people were people, on whichever side and at whichever frontier they found themselves. And it is all the more frightful when, against a background of tears, sorrow and the deaths of thousands of people and of groans and cries for help coming from the untouched ruins, I heard some people shouting slogans and demands for the 'liberation of Nagorno Karabakh'. Then I learnt that at that tragic moment Azerbaidzhan's offer of help was rejected. Can such people really be entrusted with the fate of a nation? Truly – if a blind man leads a blind man both will fall into the abyss.

I remember how, during an interval at the 4th Congress of People's Deputies of the USSR in December 1990, I was surrounded in the foyer of the Palace of Congresses. As usual there were questions and replies, arguments and discussion. Then suddenly a young, good-looking man said at the very top of his voice:

'Raisa Maksimovna, everybody is putting down the Russians, can't you see? They are humiliating our nation, they have robbed us and brought us to our knees . . .'

I had difficulty in interrupting him:

'What are you talking about? Stop and think about it for a moment. After all, it's from others that we hear that Russians like to be seen as the bosses, that they are lazy, not used to working and only exploit other people. Just think about what you are saying. One more step and we shall be looking for enemies. Who are they – these Georgians, Armenians, Estonians, Lithuanians, Jews, Kazakhs and Azerbaidzhanians – are they enemies? History has shown us more than once what that means. Or is other people's experience always just theory? The strength of the Russian people lies in the fact that we have never exploited anybody. We have never lived at the expense of other peoples. We have shared the joy of victory and the bitterness of tragedy with all the peoples of our country. And that is not a sign of weakness or of our humiliation but, I repeat, of our strength, our morality.

'Remember Dostoevsky: "I am only saying that the Russian heart is perhaps, among all the nations, the one best suited for universal, worldwide unity . . ."'

These are anxious times, with much to be concerned about. About the future of the country, about the fate of the Union of peoples, and about everything that has been created in centuries of life together. Where did this all-destructive aggressiveness spring from? When fifty- and sixty-year-old men who have been for thirty years expounding the theoretical necessity for barrack-room socialism and its superiority and have been in charge of building that society – when they announce that they will gladly destroy it all and set about its destruction, I feel scared. Are we to have more Herostratoses in our country's history? Have we really not become wiser and not rid ourselves of the fatal virus of mutual destruction? Is every policy ineffective in the face of this evil? And, generally,

Mikhail Sergeyevich's father
Sergei Andreyevich

With Mikhail Sergeyevich's mother, Maria Panteleyna,
in Privolnoye, the town where he was born

Mikhail Gorbachev as a student
in Moscow, 1953

Zdenek Mlynar, a Czech Communist who
studied in Moscow in the 1950s and
became a close friend of Mikhail
Gorbachev. He was later one of the leaders
of the 'Prague Spring' in 1968

Lida and I under one
umbrella, 1982

My daughter Irina at the age of three

Anatoli, my son-in-law, with Ksenia,
my first granddaughter

With daughter Irina
and granddaughters
Ksenia and Anastasia

Granddaughters Ksenia
and Anastasia

At the Prikumsk plastics factory in the Stavropol region, of which Mikhail Gorbachev became Party leader in 1970

The steppes and mountains of the Stavropol region have some of the most beautiful views I have ever seen

On holiday in 1976 with Yuri Andropov, who
was head of the KGB until 1982, when he became
General Secretary. Already a sick man, he died in
February 1984

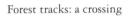

Forest tracks: a crossing

Our 'photographer' Yuri Andropov

With Alexsei Kosygin, Soviet Prime Minister 1964–80, photographed here in 1972

A meeting of the management of the Soviet Culture Fund, 1987

Above: Georgia, 1982 – with Eduard Shevardnadze, who was Soviet Foreign Minister from July 1985 until December 1990

Left: Night: collective work, collective thoughts

Below: On the banks of the Yenisei river, 1988

The children of Hungary, 1986

The republican hospital for children in Moscow

American schoolchildren in the Kremlin, 1989

Exhibition of Beam
porcelain –
with Mrs Beam,
Moscow 1987

With Svatoslav Rorich, a
Russian artist now living
in India who plans to
found a museum of his
work in Moscow

Leningrad, the Drama
Theatre, 1987

The American musical
Sophisticated Lady in
Moscow, 1988

With painter
Michael Shemyakin,
Moscow 1991

An encounter with classmates, 1990

With Natalia Sats, 1987

Geneva, 1985

With Signor Andreotti during a state visit to Italy in 1989

With Denis and Margaret Thatcher at Chequers in Britain, 1984

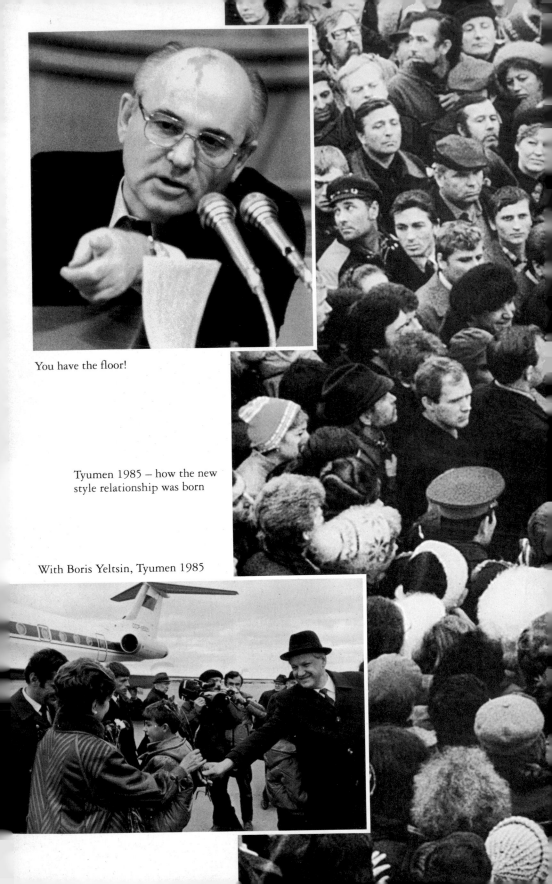

You have the floor!

Tyumen 1985 – how the new
style relationship was born

With Boris Yeltsin, Tyumen 1985

My husband meets the people of Lithuania in 1990

Czechoslavakia, 1987

must one destroy in order to move forwards? It is contrary to common sense! I am convinced that people can be happy only by being constructive.

What are the sources of this passion for besmirching the historical monuments of your own people and the tendency to present the whole seventy-year history of the Soviet period as a story of nothing but mistakes, crimes and shame? And it's not just a matter of the writing of history. How many of them have emerged recently – people pretending to be supporters of *perestroika* who are building a career, their personal well-being and their prosperity by trampling on the dignity of their country, their own people and their own history.

What is happening at times with the traditions of our intelligentsia? Or have we hastened to dispose of those traditions like second-hand books? Some intellectuals have preferred hatred to them. They preferred the all-destructive passion of hatred or they preferred to appease their conscience with such sayings as: revolutions are always started by intellectuals, carried out by fanatics and the fruits are harvested by rogues.

So I want to tell people to stop and think. Culture is both an intellectual phenomenon and a moral one. And, as I personally understand it, democracy exists so that, together and jointly, we can seek paths for the progress of society and the most effective ways to organize human life, and not so that we can fight and destroy each other. Democracy is, of course, valuable in itself, but it is still primarily an instrument for the creation of something more important. Or are we not able to live without enemies? An opposition has not yet taken shape in our country, but we already hear the cry: roll up your sleeves, draw up lists of reliable and unreliable people, appoint 'our' people and 'our' prosecutor and demolish the constitutional organs of power.

How difficult the battle has turned out to be with the times in which we lived and which formed us! Intolerance towards other people's opinions, which penetrated society in the past, is spreading today into ever new forms of hatred, struggle and confrontation. 'Raving democrats' on the one hand and 'raving conservatives' on the other. In practice the two extremes turn out to be one and the same.

I remember some episodes at the 28th Party Congress, the Russian constituent Party conference, and the April joint meeting of the Central Committee and the Control Commission. The Party recognised and supported its leader in the belief that the country could not continue to live as it had in the past. But it appears that for some people – and quite a lot of them! – it would be nice to live and change, but without really changing, without accepting changes in the way of life, the new conditions and demands, and without reacting to them. And again the same attacks, the same aggressiveness and the same moral 'execution' of the initiators of *perestroika*.

During the 28th Party Congress a newspaper called *The 13th Microphone* was published. It interviewed Mikhail Sergeyevich and published what he said. I want to quote an extract.

'How much sleep have you had in the last few days?'
'I can't sleep: even in my sleep the conflicts continue.'
'What has pained you most at the Congress?'
'I have already spoken about that. I don't like flattery:
I never have, since I was young. My friends from my
student years know that. On top of that I can't bear
brazen aggressiveness, which unfortunately was evident at
the Congress. That was very hard to endure. There was
a tendency to turn the Congress into a kangaroo court
– that was terrible and upset me more than anything.'
'And what gave you most pleasure in these days?'
'However difficult it was, good sense is prevailing.'

I remember our trip last year to Spain: Madrid, Barcelona, the El Oriente palace, the palace of Zarzuela, the Olympics complex, the Complutens university and the Institute of Soviet

Science and Culture. The Prado museum – Spain's treasure house. Picasso's *Guernica* hangs there. A lot is said about the anti-Fascist essence of that painting. But I took it to be not only a symbol of Fascism but also a symbol of war in its most frightful form in history – a symbol of the horrors of civil war. Civil war! The painting is a summons to people to return to reason. Spain lived through a civil war, and the totalitarian Franco regime lasted nearly forty years. Many of us remember how, in the 1930s, we welcomed Spanish orphans snatched from the hell of a civil war. Thousands of them found shelter in our country. And they found a second mother among our Soviet women. Now the Spanish people have found in themselves the strength and the courage to leave dictatorship behind and to set out on the path of democratic development without resorting to war, but achieving it through popular agreement.

Our historical dramas are in many ways similar, perhaps that is why we found so much understanding and so many friends on our visit to Spain. They include King Juan Carlos I, Queen Sofia and the socialist Prime Minister Gonzales, about whom my husband said after their meeting: 'Our talk together went on a long time: we had a most interesting discussion and came to some very important conclusions . . .' Another friend is Señor Villapalos, a professor of law, a leading scholar and rector of the Complutens university. And there are the Spanish children whom we took in in 1937 and who have now returned home. So many of them came up to me, and they all asked what they could do practically to help our country.

Perestroika is often described as a revolution. If it is one then it is practically unprecedented in Russia, a country of revolutions, because the main task Mikhail Sergeyevich has set himself is to carry it through democratically, without bloodshed or the use of force. Unfortunately, there have been some casualties in the years of *perestroika*. But, believe me, they would be incomparably greater in number if some forces

succeed in making the President of the country to abandon
the stand which he has taken up and defends quite consciously,
resolutely and courageously. In the words of Maksimilian
Voloshin:

> Both here and there in the ranks
> Is heard the selfsame cry:
> Who's not with us is against us,
> And justice is on *our* side.
> But I stand alone among them
> Amidst the roaring flames and smoke,
> And with all the strength I have
> I pray for one and all.

*Very much to the point! And, unless I am mistaken, written in
1919.*

In the vortex of political conflict today there is, in my view,
yet another dangerous thing taking place: society has become
excessively politicized.

I believe that, in these conditions of total politicization,
adults have the obligation as never before to be attentive to
the spiritual vitamins that our children are now being given.
I am sure of this: after all, we are now harvesting the fruit of
the childhood of generations who grew up on images and the
condemnation of 'traitors' and 'enemies of the people'. That is
why it is now so important to protect children from the influence of political passions and not to force them to be on one
side or the other of the barricades.

It is alarming and frightening to see columns of schoolchildren and adolescents at rallies calling 'down with' this or
that. It is frightening to see our children's minds filled with
those same images of 'enemies of the people' even if they are
now 'modern' enemies.

I have already told you once that I find it very sad and
disturbing that, for example, the wife of a popular people's

deputy informs us with pride in an interview published in *Ogonyok* magazine that her young daughter can tell intuitively by the look of someone appearing on television and by the way the person speaks whether he or she is one of 'ours' or is 'our' enemy. And I share the view of the author Anatoli Aleksin, President of the Soviet association Peace for the World's Children, which he outlined in the paper *Soviet Culture*: 'The seeds of enmity and hatred, of nationalism and chauvinism that are being scattered today in children's minds will never produce anything good and will never result in decent behaviour or internationalism. We are hurling the tragedy and confrontation, the burden and filth of the past, into the future, into our common tomorrow.'

Your husband's credo, which he has frequently stated, is a combination of politics and morality. What is your attitude to this supertask? Do you not regard it as idealistic?

Yes, Mikhail Sergeyevich likes to repeat that the interests of millions of people are the big issues in politics. Politics must be moral. Is that idealism? What if we try to see the larger picture?

I remember a conversation I had in the course of Mrs Thatcher's first official visit to Moscow. At dinner I asked the British Prime Minister, an outstanding politician:

'Mrs Thatcher, I would like to ask you as an ordinary person: is it moral to defend the idea that it is essential to preserve nuclear weapons on this Earth?' She replied:

'You are an idealist, Mrs Gorbachev.'

I defended myself, saying: 'But there are many idealists like me and I'm sure there will be a lot more.'

I recalled that conversation recently, following the tragedy of the war in the Persian Gulf. I attach extraordinary value to and I respect the American people's feelings of patriotism. Nevertheless I dare to say that that war, like every other, was a tragedy. I recalled the conversation with Mrs Thatcher after

hearing a major political leader of a certain state say: very well,
if force alone is effective then we shall manufacture our own
nuclear weapon. So what is that? What do you call that? No
– no war, not even to punish an aggressor, is a good thing.
Today people must learn to take into account each others'
interests, if only for the sake of their own survival. I do not
believe that, in this system of coordinates, the point where
politics and simple human morality intersect is only idealism.
No!

No, it is here, at the point of intersection of politics and
morality that we have the sources and the foundations of the
finest and most productive results of contemporary politics.

*Mikhail Sergeyevich is being accused of not making a decisive break
and not cutting off his attachment and obligations to people, and
especially to those comrades-in-arms with whom he set out on this path
of reform.*

Again, just think about it: is it really so bad? Is a purely
pragmatic and opportunistic approach to circumstances and
people so very moral?

I do not deny it: there are sometimes, it is true, bitter
lessons to be learned. For example, if fate had not handed us
the burden of *perestroika* I would probably never have known
the many different shapes and forms human beings can take.
This is serious, you understand. For me this is one of the
most difficult moral tests of *perestroika*: the specific way people
behave, what they say and what they do. What they were
yesterday and what they are today. What they are when they
are with you, and what they are with other people. What they
are when it is their advantage, and what they are when it is
not. Sometimes I even see, or rather feel, that they are not
faces but masks, but masks of the real world, not the fantastic
world of fairy-tales. And, do you know, the masks I see will
suddenly disappear and I can see quite clearly the faces of the
people who informed on my grandfather in the 1930s. And of

those who destroyed him. And of those who, with their tails between their legs, would not approach a dying woman, just because she was from the family of an 'enemy of the people'.

Nikolai Gubenko, minister of culture, actor and director, once said to me: 'Do you know what I dream of doing? I would like to make a film called "How I was a minister".' I believe there will be more than one film, but not fictional, not the result of someone's sick fantasy or inflamed imagination. They will be documentary films telling the truth about the people of *perestroika*. Fortunately, the documentary material for them, both official and unofficial, written and oral, well known and so far little known, is more than sufficient.

I think most often and with most regret, of course, about those who were comrades and colleagues of Mikhail Sergey-evich and called themselves 'brothers-in-arms'.

No, I would drop that expression.

Well, why . . . [*she shrugged her shoulders*] – that's what they called themselves. And they put a lot of effort into *perestroika*.

The ordeals that each of them went through in their careers were not easy. But did they all turn out to be up to the task; could every one of them say, hand on heart, that we were, we are and we shall continue to be part of the campaign for *perestroika*, working for our common cause?

I re-read this handwritten letter from Stanislav Sergeyevich Shatalin to Mikhail Sergeyevich and I so want to believe what he writes! The letter was written a year ago.

Dear Mikhail Sergeyevich!

I learned with bitterness and an indomitable desire to fight on about what took place at the Plenum. You know that I don't like paying compliments to my superiors. But I want to tell you that I respect you and am sincerely fond of you and am ready to go with you to the end. Don't pay any attention to the 'right-wingers'.

By virtue of a profound historical misunderstanding they
consider themselves to be communists, but they are in
fact political opportunists who have no right to speak in
the name of the people. Life will discard them and the
people will talk of them with scorn. Pay no attention
either to the hysterics of the 'Left-radicals'. Not in the
plebeian sense, but in the real sense of the word, I am
perhaps one of the most 'left' people in the USSR. But
you are carrying out on the whole the only realistic
programme for the salvation of genuine socialism and of
our country. If you want to know my opinion about ways
of investing your programme with a more consistent
character, I will be glad to oblige. Make a show of calm
and decisiveness at the Congress of Deputies. It is your
main support. Lenin was not afraid to conclude the
treaty of Brest-Litovsk. React philosophically to the
irresponsible decision of the Lithuanian Communist
Party. On January 3rd I shall return from a trip abroad
(I am preparing a major long-term project on East–West
relations) and I am ready to perform any tasks you may
give me. May these words help, however slightly, to
improve your mental equilibrium. Convey my sincere
greetings to Raisa Maksimovna. I wish you and your
family a happy New Year. We have no choice: we shall
prevail.

　　　Yours ever, Academician Stanislav Sergeyevich
Shatalin.

Here's a photograph with us all together. The photographer
was corresponding member of the Soviet Academy of Science
Georgi Khosroyevich Shakhnazarov. According to him the
great merit of the photo lies in the fact that nobody has another
like it: news photographers are not as a rule invited into such
a narrow circle, even in the time of *glasnost*.
　Yes, today *perestroika* is probably going through its period

of greatest strain. Various contradictory and totally opposed processes and forces have become interwoven. And in the centre of this gigantic whirlwind is the President of the USSR and General Secretary of the Central Committee of the CPSU and the person closest to me. Will we be able to come out of the whirlwind with honour; will we be able to create a life worthy of modern man, to revive the best that is in us and preserve the best that is around us?

Mikhail Sergeyevich lives in a state of incredible tension. Six years of daily, selfless work, in the fullest sense of the word. The years have merged into one endless working day. I never see him back home before ten or eleven o'clock at night. And he always arrives home with a pile of papers. He often works till two and sometimes three o'clock in the morning.

On foreign trips his programmes are extremely compressed and intense. Talks, the signing of documents, dozens of meetings and events − everything worked out to the hour, to the last minute of his stay in the country. Members of delegations, newspaper men and other people accompanying him on trips know it very well. He never manages to sleep more than four or five hours a night during such trips. In addition one has to bear in mind his physical state because of the changes of climate and the different time zones. Moreover, Mikhail Sergeyevich has never allowed himself the luxury of having, not just a day or two, but even a few hours for him to adapt to new conditions after a long flight.

I have noticed that foreign trips now take place mostly on a Saturday or Sunday. Previously the time taken by such trips was measured in days; now they are measured in hours. In Spain he spent thirty hours; in Italy six or seven.

That's correct. But the amount that is squeezed into such visits increases in geometric progression. Even during his holiday he practically never succeeds in cutting himself off from work. It is on holiday that he always writes his main forthcoming speeches. That was how he wrote his book on *perestroika*. And, most important, never for a minute, wherever he is, does he lose contact with Moscow. I calculated that in August 1990, in the twenty days' holiday he managed to get in Yalta, he had an average of seventeen urgent, pressing, telephone calls every day.

It was then, just before the end of our holiday, that Mikhail Sergeyevich said to me: 'We've got the most difficult time ahead of us. There is going to be political fighting . . . political squabbles . . . it's very alarming . . . You see, it will inevitably affect the economic situation and the solution of our economic problems. Our super-problem today is that we mustn't give in to the conservatives: we would never get out of that. But we mustn't surrender the fate of the country and its future to cowboys. They would ruin everything. We shall carry on step by step. Perhaps not every step will be the right one; they won't all hit the target. But they have to be taken!'

I know the pain and concern that he is going through. It is not easy, it is never easy for an honest man. It is doubly so for a man who has taken upon himself such a burden of responsibility for his country and his people. A man who is aware of his debt to people's faith, a humanist and a democrat by nature, equally exposed and receptive to people's happiness and sorrow.

Your husband has enviable self-possession. What is his secret?

People often speak of his self-control and his tolerance. But for other people – and there are some like that – it has nothing to do with self-possession but rather 'a lack of decisiveness'. Those are the people who, with provocative intentions, declare that policy is not made with shaky hands. Those are dangerous people, thrown up to the surface by our stormy times. But let us return to your question. I once heard Mikhail Sergeyevich reply to that question himself. It was in Finland at a lunch given by Mr Koivisto. In a sort of joking way Mikhail Sergeyevich then gave three 'reasons'. The first was that he had to thank his parents for having handed down to him the genetic capacity for self-control. As the second reason he named me. I have to thank Raisa Maksimovna, he said, for her help, support and loyalty. The third was his faith in the correctness of the path he had chosen and the aim he had set himself.

I believe, Georgi Vladimirovich, that the third reason is the most important: his sense of the justice, importance and necessity of what was started in 1985. What can deprive a strong man of his courage is, in my view, above all the loss of faith and doubts about its truth. I think that's it.

You know, he repeated practically the same view in a recent very frank and informal interview on Soviet television.

Yes, you are right. And I, of course, also watched and heard that interview. I will not conceal the fact that I was very pleased that, among the three reasons he gave for his self-possession he again named me – he didn't forget me. I would add to the factors named by Mikhail Sergeyevich one more which is essential for an understanding, as you say, of his self-possession, tolerance and self-control. It is very important. For him all people are human beings and personalities. He never asserts his own dignity by trampling on the dignity of other people. That has been a characteristic of him throughout his life. Never in his life has he humiliated the people next to him so as to make himself taller. Never.

And it is because of that that you hear him say things like: 'You can't agree with everything he says, of course, but he's a working man', 'he has his own opinion' and so forth. Or – 'one must, of course, give it some thought', 'there is something reasonable in all that'. Or – 'in principle we could accept it.'

This is not a case of diplomatic etiquette, and certainly not of timidity, indecisiveness or uncertainty. And not even of any special upbringing. It is an inborn respect for human beings, about which I have spoken. You know, in the family he listens to everyone as an equal, from the eighty-year-old to the three-year-old.

I have no doubts about Mikhail Sergeyevich's moral strength. My worries concern something else, and I think millions of women, wives and mothers, will understand me. I am extremely worried today about his health.

I would like to bring this meeting to an end, Georgi Vladimirovich, by answering your question: what do I understand by happiness? It is very simple and very complicated. It is an eternal question, one as complex and as many-sided as life itself. I know one thing: you can't be happy if you are alone – if nobody needs you.

I have in front of me a message of congratulation on the occasion of Women's Day, the 8th of March, which I have just received.

Dear Raisa Maksimovna,

However hard it is for you and Mikhail Sergeyevich in these desperate times you may rest assured that the efforts made in the last six years to transform and improve our country have given it a simpler, more sincere image, in harmony with the concepts of honesty, morality and humanity. It is difficult, even impossible in the course of six years to bring the process of *perestroika* to completion. But I know that all your thoughts, and all your feelings and all that you have done together in these years had only one aim – to serve the country. Nikolai Gubenko.

The second is a note from Georgi Khosroyevich Shakhnazarov.

Dear Raisa Maksimovna,

I send you my heartfelt congratulations on the 8th of March. An amazing fate has befallen you – both a happy one and in some ways an unkind one. But you are taking both its gifts and its blows with great human dignity. If marriages are really made in heaven God tried to give Mikhail Sergeyevich a companion in life in accordance with the mission he was destined for.

Yours sincerely, Shakhnazarov.

Perhaps that *is* happiness, Georgi Vladimirovich? Or . . .

Here is one of the gifts that I hold very dear – *Vanity Fair* by Thackeray. It's a first edition, published in London in 1848. It was presented to me by Mrs Margaret Thatcher. This work of an outstanding novelist ends with the question: 'Which of us is happy in this world?'

The work was finished. I was escorted downstairs, right to the front porch where a car was awaiting, and I kissed my hostess's hand. She remained at the porch where there was also a feeling of spring. The house behind her was lit up only in places: no expensive illuminations. Before walking to the car I tried to impress the picture on my memory: the house, the glass door and the woman standing on the threshold.

Yes, I had read that in the West Raisa Gorbachev had been described as 'the Kremlin's secret weapon', thus suggesting that personal charm is also capable of producing entirely tangible political dividends. But I cannot get out of my head the scene I witnessed outside the miners' club in Donetsk: in a friendly way Raisa Gorbachev takes by the hand a woman, apparently a working woman, who wants to say something but just can't push her way through to where the top people are, and leads her into the circle of heated political and industrial discussion. I can't get it out of my head probably because that scene was repeated so often before my very eyes. Not only in Donetsk, not only in Sverdlovsk, or in Nizhny Tagil.

And so I am now thinking on my way back into Moscow: and in the Kremlin itself? Whose 'weapon' is she in the Kremlin itself? – for it is certainly a fact that even there she is not just a porcelain figure.

Today, when I know more about Raisa Gorbachev than anyone

else outside her immediate circle, the answer to that question is clearer to me. However elegant, and even refined, she may be in the corridors of power, humanizing them in her way and making them more attractive, smarter and even more interesting for the public at large, she is invisibly accompanied, it seems to me, by the hardships of her childhood, the blind cripples singing not very soberly on railway platforms after the war, and by the woman from a miners' area harassed by our current humiliating shortages and disarray. If Raisa Gorbachev is known in the West as a 'weapon of the Kremlin', it seems to me that in the Kremlin itself she is a 'weapon' for those who have no weapons. May God grant it!

I recently read somewhere a very interesting report. A group of specialists made a study of the contemporary popular idea of female beauty — only I don't know what kind of specialists they were — in female beauty or statistics. They collected the facts together, studied them and arrived at some generalizations that were really startling. The ideal turned out to be the average. A face made up of exactly the average nose, the most ordinary lips, eyebrows, and so forth. Symmetry rules, not only over the real world, but also over our imagination, it appears. The less individuality there is the greater the attraction. Is there anything wrong with individuality — at least in the popular idea of beauty?

In Russia, out of a sense of self-preservation, the wife of the top leader usually did not step a millimetre outside his shadow. The more she kept in the shadow the better.

Raisa Gorbachev deliberately keeps away from any part of the official power structure: if she plays any part it is only in social work and even then not in a prominent role. I cannot say that she ever oversteps the political boundaries set by her husband, or speaks out of turn. She does not, and she is extremely careful in that. It seems to me that even the rhythm of her speech, especially on television, is conditioned not only by her many years' work as a teacher but also by a strict inner self-control.

The boundaries coincide, and all the same you can see a quite obvious, strange luminescence round the edges. True, I would not call

*this the Raisa Gorbachev phenomenon but the Gorbachevs' phenom-
enon. She permits herself an individuality, expressed primarily in a
sense of her own worth, while he treats that feeling with invariable
quiet respect. That is their phenomenon — the phenomenon of the
preservation of individuality.*

*I have noticed that she doesn't like the empty chatter of society. She
keeps the thread of any conversation firmly in her hands. She reacts
sympathetically when you hit upon the right word or some worthwhile
thought, but when something you say is off-target, she reacts with
even greater sharpness. Altogether the woman whose book you are now
reading is not one of those with whom you can relax mentally when
you are talking — it is as well to keep the mind in good working
condition.*

*She is also a woman who does not turn her eyes away from the
truth: to know nothing, see nothing, hear nothing. She does not turn
away, and she prefers to call a spade a spade. I am not sure whether,
for all the President's democratic ways, there are many people in the
top Soviet establishment who are telling him the direct truth. But
that she is one of them, of that I am convinced because I heard it said
more than once. Even though it is probably more painful and more
difficult for her than for anybody else to voice that straight truth.*

*There may sometimes be salvation in a lie. It seems to me that she
believes that only the truth, however bitter it may be, can be salutary.
That corresponds more with her character and her past.*

CHAPTER SIX

My Hopes

I am writing these concluding lines of the book late in the evening. Vremya, *the main news programme on Soviet television, has just ended. It included an item having direct relation to my last meeting with Raisa Gorbachev. Directing my attention to a pile of letters and telegrams sent to her husband on his sixtieth birthday, she had said:*

And one fellow, a pensioner and beekeeper from the Ukraine, apparently sent Mikhail Sergeyevich a ton of honey as a gift.

Why 'apparently'?

Well, I received notification – we had to take delivery of a ton of honey. I thought: they've probably made a mistake. Instead of a kilogram someone has written a 'ton'.

Let's tell the story of the honey in the book – it's interesting.

I'm not sure about that; in any case we ought to make quite sure: maybe it really was some kind of mistake.

Judging by the report that appeared in the Vremya *programme, it was not a mistake. Raisa Gorbachev took the honey to an old folks' home. She sat there among them, chatting, replying to questions and for good company drank tea with the honey that had been redirected to the home on her husband's instructions. I know that another Presidential gift had found a place in that Moscow home for the elderly: a luxurious television set that Li Peng presented to Mikhail Gorbachev in Peking and which Gorbachev ordered to be handed over to the old folk.*

I had learnt earlier that day that there had been no mistake about the honey when I happened to run into the person whom the President had instructed to deliver some of the honey to a children's home that treated children who had cerebral illnesses and had been rejected by their parents at birth.

The 'Presidential honey' was in fact divided into three parts: for the children's home, for the old folks' home, and for the Moscow children's Republican hospital, of which, as has already been said, Mrs Gorbachev is a patron.

In general the conclusion of the book and a postscript to it should by rights be written by the author herself – Raisa Gorbachev. But I am writing these lines especially since seeing on the screen the concentrated and self-controlled features of the person I had only recently been talking to, and hearing her, in words so unusual for her and for Soviet television in general, send Easter greetings to the old folk.

These are difficult, even bitter, times for the President. Perhaps the Ukrainian beekeeper is a distant descendant of that same Rudy Panko about whom Gogol wrote his unforgettable Evenings on a Farm near Dikanka *and in his simplicity does not himself suspect how symbolic his sincere gift was.*

Raisa Gorbachev has already explained why she decided to produce this book. The book is an explanation of her own self and, while addressing herself to the foreign reader, she of course sees out of the corner of her eyes our own, Russian reader. Who knows – perhaps it is actually a try-out before writing a book directed exclusively at the Soviet public? She wants to be understood in her own country. I saw, when she decided to write this book, that Raisa Gorbachev had to step beyond the limits of her own character, her own reserved nature, and ultimately of tradition. Unless my memory lets me down, only one Soviet 'first lady', that being Nadezhda Krupskaya, has ever undertaken anything like it. She acted contrary to tradition, although it is precisely for ignoring some of this country's oldest traditions that

*she is most often criticized. To be understood means to a certain extent
to be supported.*

*I am impressed as a person by the sincere impulse that motivates
Raisa Gorbachev. Moreover I am profoundly convinced that, for all
Mikhail Gorbachev's exclusivity, he is not an accidental but a completely logical and necessary figure in our contemporary history. And
his exclusivity is probably in the fact that he has detected with unusual
sharpness the general direction in which things were moving — from
a world that is breaking up and divided and fraught with the prospect
of self-destruction to the concept of a single world — and the latent
readiness of society to move in this direction; he injected into that
movement an* exclusive *tempo — with all the associated consequences.
He did so also because he realized that he had very little time left.*

*As I was re-reading V. O. Klyuchevsky I came across the fact that
Peter the Great, the most resolute and dramatic reformer of Russia,
ruled the country for thirty-six years. He became Tsar in 1682 and
ruled from 1689 to 1725. That's how many years it appears are
needed in Russia for achieving cardinal reforms! Gorbachev realized
that he would not have thirty-six years of* rule, *if only because it
was not for that that he made a final break with Stalinism.*

*All of us in this country are waiting for him to produce results —
'here and now'. As the father of four children, despite the general
and quite natural impatience, I would agree: let our children enjoy
the results, so long as they come. Regard this as the pardonable
digression of a reporter in the unfamiliar field of political general-
ization.*

Now I hand over the microphone to Raisa Gorbachev:

So, Georgi Vladimirovich, today we have our sixth and
final meeting, as you and I agreed. Were they conversations,
interviews or just time for recollections? I don't know. You
will remember that I did not agree at once to do them. Why?
I have spoken about that at the beginning of the book; that
was where we started.

Mikhail Sergeyevich and I are very fond of ballads. Perhaps

that is typical of our generation – I don't know. Amongst the ballads we like most is one of which a recording can often be heard in our home, an old Russian love song by A. Abaza to the words of Turgenev. It is almost the only love song Turgenev wrote. It is sung by Nikolai Gedda – 'A misty morning, a grey morning, the mournful fields covered in snow.' It's a beautiful love song! As for Gedda's voice, I don't even know what adjective to choose: beautiful, enchanting, magical or amazing. A love song puts you in the mood for recollecting. His hero himself recollects. But, Georgi Vladimirovich, our life with its daily affairs, problems and cares, and our hours, days and years full to bursting – has no time for reminiscences.

I have heard Mikhail Sergeyevich say many times: 'I always wanted and I still want to write. But there has never been time for it and there still isn't.' As for me, I was beset by doubts: ought I to give interviews and talk about myself – why? Or talk about Mikhail Sergeyevich? But no one can talk about him, what he has been through and is still going through, better and more truly, than he can himself. About what he has done and how and why. But in life there is on every side a 'division of labour': some people do things; others write about them and criticize. Everyone has his own destiny. But that is by the way.

And now, Georgi Vladimirovich, I do not regret having had these talks with you. I don't regret it, although these four months – as far as I recall our first meeting was some time at the end of December last year – these four months have proved to be for me physically, intellectually and emotionally difficult. It was also because they coincided with a grave, perhaps the most difficult, period in the life of our country and in Mikhail Sergeyevich's work. And because, for the first time in my life, I came to a halt, so to speak, and relived my own life. I have been trying to recall facts and events from my past. And, quite unexpectedly for me, out of some quite unthinkable depths of my memory, these episodes, happenings and facts from my past began to roll out like little beads and link up, string themselves together and turn into a very long, endless thread of reminiscences. Such an experience probably happens in every person's life.

I have discovered that there is a great deal more that I want to talk about: about my family, about the people with whom my life is linked and about what I have seen. And about the letters that people send me. Previously it never occurred to me to talk about these things.

And again. It turned out emotionally not to be so easy to deal with this avalanche of reminiscences. I really did seem to be living through it all over again. As I told you, I wept as I recalled this or that event and my heart ached. I lived through it all again in those four months.

Finally I tried to understand and work out the meaning of what happened and what is happening now. That is also very important for me. These four months included so many extra-ordinary events and so many very important decisions. So many changes took place in the country and in ourselves. It was a truly critical and crucial period.

Perestroika is not a barren fig-tree: there is fruit on it. But there are also bad things that it has exposed or perhaps itself caused involuntarily. I dream of the time when they will no longer exist, when *perestroika* will begin to yield tangible and rich harvests, so that everybody will feel – and this is the most important for me – that they are inwardly more at peace with themselves, that it is firmer underfoot, and better both at table and at home. I want my husband, along with his supporters and associates, to carry what they have started to a successful conclusion and to see for themselves the real fruits of the tremendous transformation they have undertaken.

I want particularly to say something about my husband's colleagues, about the people who initiated the changes with him and who are now still at his side, battling along together through all the obstacles, mistakes and prejudices. There are among them people whom I know well and there are others whom I know less well, who are younger and who set out later on this thorny path so necessary for the country and society. But I am grateful to every one of them for the active help they have given my husband and their loyalty to the common cause. I wish all of them well. I wish them and their families not to give up and not to lose the strength of spirit that is nourished by the importance of the cause they are serving.

The stabilization of the market for consumer goods, of the monetary system, the land reform, the beginnings of phasing out state control and free enterprise are gathering force. If they are not upset by political cataclysms we have the right to expect change for the better. And the sooner the better!

On the 13th of March 1991 our country held the first referendum in its history. Eighty per cent of the Soviet citizens registered on the electoral roll went to the polls to answer the question: 'Do you consider it necessary to preserve the Union of Soviet Socialist Republics as a renewed federation of equal sovereign republics in which the rights and freedoms of persons of any nationality will be fully guaranteed?' To this, 76.4 per cent said: 'Yes, let there be a great, renewed, democratic Soviet Union.'

I believe and hope that Soviet people will have the strength, self-control and patriotism and – I consider this very important – the common sense to overcome all the difficulties and obstacles on the path to such an end. I would like the Soviet Union, while passing through the crucible of renewal, to remain a union – of peoples, republics and ideals. We cannot allow to be cast to the winds the priceless, centuries-old moral and social experience of so many scores of languages and peoples living together and collaborating. It seems to me that that experience will still be of value to everyone, the whole of human civilization. Who knows – perhaps it is precisely that centuries-old mutual attraction and interpenetration that constitutes what in olden days they called an 'emanation of the

spirit' – from every one of the peoples inhabiting the Union
– including the Russian people?

My hope is for peace. There is nothing more frightful or
more inhuman than war. The calamity of war, wherever,
whenever and upon whomever it descends, is a tragedy for the
whole of humanity. Only a few years back practically every
time Mikhail Sergeyevich met with the people you could hear
the cry: 'So long as there's no war!' And in the 1960s and
1970s even I, still a very young woman sociologist going with
my questionnaires from one village house to another, would
be asked anxiously, especially by mothers of children: 'And
there will be no war?' I would ask them about their pay, their
work, their children, their families and their needs, about
how often they visited the cinema, the club or friends – the
questionnaire included such questions – and they would reply:
'So long as there's not a war!' Nowadays such cries and such
fundamental questions are not heard. The threat of a worldwide conflagration, threat of annihilation, that was felt keenly
for decades by every home in our country and every family,
has been averted. For my country, which has for centuries been
at the junction of two worlds, that is a change in its perception
of the world and its attitude towards it: from a constant state
of anxiety to the acquisition of a sense of security.

The world is no longer split in two. For Russia, for the
Soviet Union and for all the peoples on this Earth peace has
become more durable. I am proud of this because, after all, it
is to a large extent thanks to the political efforts and statesman-
ship of my husband. I am proud of the Nobel Peace Prize he
was awarded. I am, of course, worried, very worried, lest there
should develop a confrontational situation within our country.
Such a conflict, destructive and senseless, could develop into
a tragedy not only for our people but for the whole of humanity. In a peaceful future lies the happiness and well-being of
the people of this Earth, the happiness of our country, our

children and grandchildren, including the President's family
too.

March has just come to an end. It is a special month in
Mikhail Sergeyevich's life. In March 1985 he was elected
General Secretary of the Central Committee of the CPSU. In
March 1990 he became the country's first nationally elected
President. On the 2nd of March he celebrated his sixtieth
birthday. We received several thousand warm and much
appreciated congratulations and good wishes from all kinds of
people and from every corner of the country.

Dear Mikhail Sergeyevich.

Congratulations on your birthday. I wish you from the
bottom of my heart the very best, good health and
happiness, and steadfastness. After all, it is so terribly
difficult to be the President of our unfortunate country.
We are endlessly grateful to you for your incredible
achievement in ridding us of fear and giving us hope and
freedom. We grew up under Brezhnev and regarded
everyone at the seat of power with revulsion and hatred.
But we have faith in you. And when the nationwide
presidential election takes place we shall vote for
you.

With the most profound respect – Lev Isakovich
Sigal, Marina Valentinovna Morozova, Moscow.

Good day, Mikhail Sergeyevich.

Don't be upset because you have reached sixty. It is
not very much. Every day that you live can be compared
to years. The good seeds you have sown with your heart
and mind in our sinful land will inevitably yield a good
harvest and much joy. Where can I send you some white
dried mushrooms?

The Chakushkin family, Cheboksary.

Dear Mikhail Sergeyevich.

Sincere birthday greetings. Courage to you, dear fellow, in the struggle for justice and happiness for the people.

Communists, members of the Komsomol and Pioneers, the teachers and the whole staff of school No. 64 in Stavropol.

Dear Mikhail Sergeyevich.

I offer you my heartfelt congratulations on your sixtieth birthday. First of all I wish you good health and strength of mind. Don't give in, and don't retreat. I can see that you are having difficulties. Your political opponents, and not only the political ones, hide themselves behind democratic phraseology and are fighting a fierce battle with you and your team. They do not use only political methods. Unfortunately, they have succeeded in literally fooling a section of the population of our country, using for their mercenary ends the economic difficulties and the conflicts between the nationalities which, I am sure, arose through the fault of those 'democrats'. Once again I wish you good health, success and happiness in your private life.

Your firm supporter, Kozlov, Smolensk.

Dear Mikhail Sergeyevich.

We congratulate you from the bottom of our hearts on your sixtieth birthday. We wish you good health and success in your laborious efforts to revive our Motherland. Genuine workers are wholly on your side. We support you and have faith in you. You should know that you are our hope. We embrace and kiss you. May God help you.

Alla Karabanova and Nina Nazarova, telegraphists at the Central Post Office, Moscow.

Dear and deeply respected Mikhail Sergeyevich.

Sincere congratulations on your birthday. The very best and soundest of health to you. Please hold on in the face of lies and extremism. Sincerest compliments for your patience and courage. Remember that your nobility of character is our human hope. We support you with all our hearts.

M. Shask, Leningrad.

Dear Mikhail Sergeyevich.

I congratulate you on your birthday. I wish you good health and success in your difficult task. I would like you always to be President and to fight for peace. Come and be our guest in Petrozavodsk and we can go fishing together.

Misha Torchik, nine years old, Petrozavodsk.

Dear Mikhail Sergeyevich.

We congratulate you on your birthday and wish you success in your difficult work.

Students at Lvov State University.

There are two more letters, to which I would like to draw special attention:

Dear Mikhail Sergeyevich.

I send you warmest greetings on your birthday. In my old age fate gave me the possibility of meeting you, a person at the very centre of world events. This was exceptionally valuable for me. I regard it as a gift. Life has mixed up a great deal (but not everything!). It is difficult to shield oneself from its winds, we are all exposed. Born in the provinces of Russia, I continue to believe in the man of the soil. He is closer to heaven, and therefore

stronger, than men of the air. I send you heartfelt
greetings and wish you health, strength of will and
long life to carry out the task that has been placed on
you.

    With deep respect, Georgi Vasilyevich Sviridov [the
foremost Soviet composer].

To the President of the USSR, M. S. Gorbachev.

    Deeply respected and dear Mikhail Sergeyevich. Permit
me to congratulate you sincerely and from my heart on the
sixtieth anniversary of your birth. I pray that the Lord
may increase your strength and that your heart should
always retain its wisdom, full of peace and love. May your
work as head of the great Soviet state be blessed and
may you succeed in strengthening the unity of our peoples
in all their variety and the enrichment of each other's
life. I believe that with God's help the great cause that
you have initiated for the renewal of our Motherland on
democratic, law-based and moral principles will arrive at
its beneficent conclusion despite all difficulties. I assure
you that our prayers and our efforts are an inseparable
part of this great historical process. Please convey my
sincere congratulations to your partner in life, Raisa
Maksimovna, and all those close to you.

    With deep respect, Aleksi, Patriarch of Moscow and
All Russia.

We also received a great many flowers on his birthday. Splen-
did roses, magnificent orchids, messengers from the heart,
pinks, tulips from the steppes. Beautiful blue irises — the
colour of hope. Patches of crimson anthuriums and yellow,
lilac and white freesias. By tradition, Georgi Vladimirovich,
I give Mikhail Sergeyevich violets on his birthday. The violet
is a delicate, graceful flower that smells of the open air and
the spring. It is for us a symbol of youth and reminds us of

the first year of our married life when, for the first time after our marriage, Mikhail Sergeyevich and I travelled down to his native village. Have you come across that southern tradition – the little garden in front of the parents' cottage and the scent of night violets growing in it? From that time the violet became my invariable present.

On behalf of his mother and mine and on behalf of our children, grandchildren, brothers and sisters, and on my own behalf, of course, I said to Mikhail Sergeyevich on his sixtieth birthday: 'Thank you for the fact of your being, for being what you are, and for the fact that we are beside you.'

I hope that his health will not abandon my husband or let him down. After all, he has just turned sixty. I hope that my children and grandchildren will keep well. I hope that fate will grant me too the strength to be with them as long as possible and alongside my husband, helping him and sharing every heart-beat.

We have had everything in our life – joy and sorrow, tremendously hard work and colossal nervous strain, successes and failures, poverty, hunger and material well-being. He and I have gone through it all while still preserving the original basis of our relationship and our devotion to our ideas and ideals. I believe that strength of spirit, courage and firmness will help my husband now to withstand the unprecedented ordeals of the most difficult stage in our life.

I hope.

Moscow
December 1990 – April 1991